BIRTHINGS
and
BLESSINGS

BIRTHINGS
and
BLESSINGS

*Liberating Worship Services
for the Inclusive Church*

ROSEMARY CATALANO MITCHELL
and
GAIL ANDERSON RICCIUTI

CROSSROAD • NEW YORK

1991

The Crossroad Publishing Company
370 Lexington Avenue, New York, NY 10017

Copyright © 1991
by Rosemary Catalano Mitchell and Gail Anderson Ricciuti

Printed in the United States of America
Typesetting output: TEXSource, Houston

Library of Congress Cataloging-in-Publication Data

Mitchell, Rosemary Catalano.
    Birthings and blessings : liberating worship services for the inclusive church / Rosemary Catalano Mitchell and Gail Anderson Ricciuti.
      p. cm.
    Includes bibliographical references.
    ISBN 0-8245-1126-3
    1. Women—Prayer-books and devotions—English. 2. Liturgies.
I. Ricciuti, Gail Anderson. II. Title.
BV4844.M48 1991
264'.0082—dc20   91-15439
                                             CIP

To our foremothers in faith, past and present —
all those women whose lives have inspired and strengthened ours
across centuries or across dinner tables...

to Margee, Jean, Elayne, Madeline, Carla,
Jan, and Great Aunt Ruth,
whose vision, intelligence, and grace
call forth *our* best...

and to our husbands, Joe and Anthony,
whose strong partnership and liberated spirits
have been our encouragement...

this book is lovingly dedicated.

Contents

Acknowledgments

Our "Women, Word, and Song" gathering in Rochester, New York, from which this book has grown, is successful and life-giving because so many have participated in it. We are thankful for the support and help of these people:

Jean Brigham, Carol and Jeff Brown, Martha Brown, Joyce Button, Jane Conner, Joanne Curran, Virginia Davidson, Dr. Joanna Dewey, Karen Dragano, the Rev. Ann Evinger, Elyse Gilman, the Rev. Carol Gomez, Suzanne Goodrich, the Rev. Mary Lynn Gras, Barbara Griffiss, Kristin Hunt, Alice Ingram, Diane Jannarone, Bets and Selden Knudson, Patricia Kulaga, Doris Lasch, Mary Mohlke, Barbara Owen, Becky Parks, Ann Poland, Joanne Poland, Georgiana Prasil, Nancy Reynolds, Susan Richane, Judy Ward, Laura Woods, and Kay Wroblewski.

We are indebted to our staff colleagues who were always willing to lend a hand: Mary Ellen Britt, Dr. J. Melvin Butler, Alan Jones, Jerry Mosholder, Martha Nurenburg, and Steve Simmons and his crew.

Presbyterian Women of the Downtown United Presbyterian Church has been our partner and benefactor in this experience. We thank them for their courage and visionary thinking.

We are also appreciative of grants given by the Presbytery of Genesee Valley, the Churchwide Coordinating Team of Presbyterian Women, and the Theology and Worship Ministry Unit of the Presbyterian Church (U.S.A.), and extend our gratitude for their encouragement in this endeavor.

Our gratitude is boundless for the patience and skill of John Eagleson, our editor at Crossroad/Continuum. His wise and clearheaded guidance have been immensely helpful to us and have made him a true partner in bringing this book to birth.

Most of all, we are grateful for all the people of the Downtown United Presbyterian Church — whose life together reads like a living Gospel.

Introduction

In Margaret Atwood's novel *The Handmaid's Tale*, a repressive future society called Gilead keeps the Bible under lock and key. Only the commander of a household, a male, is permitted to read it — and then only selectively. Many portions are *never* read aloud and so have faded gradually from common memory. Women are not permitted to read at all.

The handmaid named Offred, whose stream of consciousness makes up the story's narrative, observes that "the Bible is kept locked up the way people once kept tea locked up — to keep the servants from stealing it. . . . The Bible is an incendiary device: who *knows* what we'd make of it, if we could get our hands on it."

And so it is with many women here and now who have begun to discover for ourselves a spirituality no longer kept under the lock and key of the traditional, androcentric scriptural interpretations of our childhood years in Sunday School. We are finding, as did the early church and then the church of the Reformation, the liberating and incendiary power of the Word.

The gathering called "Women, Word, and Song" had its beginning at the Downtown United Presbyterian Church, Rochester, New York, in the fall of 1987. A group of young women of the congregation who had not found a niche in traditional church women's activities were seeking opportunities to gather for Bible study, reflection, and community building. At the same time, we knew of women who had been alienated from the institutional church — some of them for long years — by their experience of the church's abuse of power or its patriarchal theology, and we longed for a way to offer an alternative model of worship and reflection that would welcome all these sisters "home" to a faith community together.

We began to realize that in spite of the rich history of suffragist and feminist ferment in our area (upstate New York) there did not exist a Protestant expression of worship that was women-directed and women-oriented as well as inclusive. We also saw a need for outreach to women who were unchurched or "formerly churched," who for many reasons no longer participated in traditional worship. The older women of the congregation were receptive to our ideas and delighted to be able to invite a wider community into involvement; and so with the blessing and sponsorship of our congregation's Presbyterian Women organization, "Women, Word, and Song" was born.

Since that time, we have met approximately every eight weeks on Sunday evenings — not in a formal "worship space" but in the church parlor. Twenty-five women attended our first gathering to participate in an early-Advent reflection on birthing. Since then, the number of women who attend "Women, Word, and Song" has tripled. They have represented congregations other than our own, members of other faiths, and those with no church affiliation whatsoever, in addition to active church members. After that first gathering we invited participants to work with us on an ad hoc basis in planning and leadership; and they have become a rich wellspring. Together, we have developed a statement of purpose that continues to inform this spiritual birthing process. It guides us "to engage women in theological reflection and Bible study to [identify] the connection between our faith and our experience; to promote the leadership...[and] to call forth the creativity of women as we explore new forms of worship; to provide alternative Christian worship experiences within the context of the local congregation for women for whom traditional worship forms have become irrelevant, meaningless, or oppressive...."

Through it all, it has become increasingly apparent to us that women are eager to reflect upon theology and spirituality with one another. We are convinced that programs like ours are vital not only to the survival of the Christian church, but to its transformation; and we hope readers will agree and catch the vision of such ministry.

Although "Women, Word, and Song" is still new among us, its roots are deep. The rich soil out of which it has sprung, in this faith community, is Celebration II. Celebration II is a contemporary experimental *and* experiential form of worship (Celebration I is Reformed worship in a more formal and traditional mode), which had its beginnings with the birth of the Downtown Church some eighteen years ago. Three downtown congregations, all within a radius of three city blocks, entered together into a thorough study/visioning process over the course of several years — deciding, as a result, to merge for the sake of wise stewardship, vital witness, and mission in the city. It was a time of tremendous excitement. Out of that creative ferment came many new ideas — including the vision of "alternative" worship each Sunday morning planned by the people, growing out of their community life, and in dialogue with Scripture. In nurturing the tender shoot from the older branch, we have learned that frontiers give birth to frontiers!

C-II, as it is called, has now journeyed and evolved through almost two decades, each Sunday morning service different from the week before and without a traditional setting, sermon, or choir. The constant, however, has been the bringing together of all ages and abilities. Through this experience, an entire congregation — including those who choose to worship exclusively in the "traditional" Celebration I — has come to accept and *expect* diversity, creative theological inquiry, and inclusiveness. And we believe that these qualities in worship and church life have nourished an excitement about the Bible as well as a maturity of faith and mission that are too often missing in many Protestant forms of worship.

Part II of this book, "Inclusive Worship for the Church Community," contains a sampling of those services: not so pointedly directed toward women as those in Part I but created for both women and men, children and adults, able-bodied and differently-abled, worshipping together in inclusive communities.

Finally, Part III is a weekend retreat that offers women an opportunity to let go of fear and claim God's gifts of power, love, and sound-mindedness.

STARTING POINTS

Our "Women, Word, and Song" gathering is rooted in feminist premises regarding worship. This is reflected in a diversity of style that stands in bold contrast to the traditional worship experience of many, if not most, churches. Common to the fabric of each of these services are foundational starting points — many of which have taken shape through the course of one congregation's life together and its commitment to the ministry of the whole people of God. We describe ten of them here, in order to offer to women and men in other faith communities a springboard for exploring creative vistas in their own worship life.

1. Corporateness and Collegiality

No single leader in the community is responsible for creating worship. Not only worshipping, but also planning, are corporate acts, so there is a fluidity of leadership. In practice this means that a different core group of women is intentionally brought together to plan each gathering.

2. The Validity of the Experiential

Our very life experience is holy! This means that nothing is forbidden for discussion in the context of worship, and that the language of worship does not necessarily have to be "worship language." In this respect, "Women, Word, and Song" is based upon the expectation that each woman has faith, wisdom, and insight worth sharing. Again, this stance enables spiritual leadership to flow back and forth throughout the worshipping community.

3. The Local Is the Universal

Although part of the richness of "Women, Word, and Song" has been its inclusion of women from a variety of backgrounds, the services have been created in the context of a specific local church and its particular faith tradition. This has been a marked contrast to most ecumenical or regional gatherings, in which the worship experience is often, of necessity, reduced to the simplest common denominator.

4. The Centrality of the Word

While women of other traditions have also created rituals, liturgies, and prayer services with roots in their own historic expression of faith, "Women, Word, and Song" intentionally springs from the Reformed tradition, in that the Word carries weight that anchors the entire service. It is our goal that the biblical text is experienced not as an *addition* to worship, but as the fertile ground out of which the full expression of worship grows. Whereas the proclamation of God's Word in terms of preaching has historically been the focus of Reformed worship, proclamation in the context of "Women, Word, and Song" takes many different forms.

5. The Sensuality of Worship

Worship invites the use of all the senses, not only the auditory. We feel it is also important to be conscious of the visual, tactile, and olfactory and to allow time for worshippers to savor these channels of spiritual nurture. Without them, worship becomes arid — cut off from its richest depths.

6. The Flexibility of "Sacred Space"

The "sacred" dimension of life is not confined exclusively to designated sanctuary spaces with standard accoutrements such as organ, pews, stained glass, and pulpit. Worship in a feminist mode blesses and finds blessing in *unexpected* space such as parlor, lounge, or entryway; where the breaking open of old expectations and visual patterns allows for the in-breaking of the Spirit — often with breathtaking insight! Each space has its own feeling and unique possibilities for eliciting both reverence and interaction.

7. The Significance of Rhythm

We have happily freed ourselves from the assumption that worship of this kind must happen every week. Instead, a more flexible rhythm has allowed us to focus our gatherings around the seasons of life and liturgy, with time for a creative process that would be excluded by rigid scheduling.

8. Variety in Worship Order

Historically, our own tradition has valued the conduct of worship "decently and in order." While maintaining respect for that principle, we also affirm that many formats can exist together in the same worshipping community. Although each "Women, Word, and Song" gathering incorporates various basic elements (song, prayer, engagement with the Word through Scripture and other writings, conversation and the sharing of life experience) the order and ways in which these are expressed vary a great deal from gathering to gathering.

9. The Surprising Role of Worship Leaders

The role of a worship leader in our celebrations contrasts with traditional expectations. To enable community members to follow the Spirit's movement among them, the leader must not so much talk as listen — at a level that, as theologian Nelle Morton wrote, will "hear them into speech." With this awareness, the leader's role is to remind the community that the Word of God does not originate from *her* but among *them*.

10. The Winds of the Spirit

Throughout this book we attempt to provide thorough and detailed notes on background, preparation, and "choreography." Although the most subtle nuances of worship in *any* style ought to be carefully considered for the sake of aesthetic beauty as well as theological coherence, nevertheless in the last analysis it is the movement of the Holy Spirit that brings the hour of worship alive. Worship leaders must maintain a sense of humor and humility about this! The printed order of worship is best viewed not as a jungle gym on which to climb up unyielding bars, but as a flying trapeze — whose fluidity demands that we often let go and trust ourselves to the "air"! "The wind blows where it wills, and you hear the sound of it, but you do not know whence it comes or whither it goes; so it is with every one [and every experience of worship] born of the Spirit" (John 3:8). The sudden emergence of insight, laughter, or tears is not viewed as disruptive to a well-ordered service, but a blessing sign. Those who learn to trust themselves to that flow will know worship as both a living and a life-giving moment!

A WORD ABOUT RESOURCES

Music plays an important role in a worship experience, and can be incorporated in many ways. If taped music is used, it is important to make sure the tape player is of a good quality and that it is well suited to the worship space. Worshippers may sing along with a tape or use the music as meditation, with the words printed in the order of worship. Flutists, guitarists, or pianists, for example, may be invited to participate. We discover that as time goes on, people offer their gifts of music in surprising ways.

Sources of music are many; but if the theme or approach will be radically new to those who gather, using familiar hymns offers a comfortable balance. We have included suggested alternate hymns at the end of each service to offer flexibility to those wishing to use more familiar or (in some cases) more accessible music.

Where special readings are used in these services, we have included the full text. However, a piece to be read by only one voice need not be printed in your order of worship.

SUGGESTED RESOURCES FOR MUSIC

Because We Are One People. The Ecumenical Women's Center, Chicago, Ill.

Creation Sings. Philadelphia: Geneva Press, 1979.

Everflowing Streams. Ruth C. Duck and Michael G. Bausch, eds. New York: Pilgrim Press, 1981.

Inclusive Language Hymns (based on *The Pilgrim Hymnal*). The First Congregational Church (Amherst, MA 01002), 1984.

New Hymns for the Lectionary. Music by Carol Doran, words by Thomas H. Troeger. New York: Oxford University Press, 1986.

Sing a WomanSong. The Ecumenical Women's Center, Chicago, Ill.

A Singing Faith, by Jane Parker Huber. Philadelphia: Westminster Press, 1987.

Songs of Hope and Peace. New York: Pilgrim Press, 1988

Songs of Shalom. Ministry of the Laity, Board of Discipleship, United Methodist Church, Nashville, Tenn., 1983

WomanPrayer, WomanSong, by Miriam Therese Winter. Oak Park, Ill.: Meyer-Stone Books, 1987; available from Crossroad Publishing Co., New York.

KEY FOR SOURCES OF SUGGESTED ALTERNATE HYMNS

HB	*The Hymnbook* (Philadelphia: Presbyterian Church, U.S., Presbyterian Church, U.S.A., and Reformed Church in America, 1955)
PH	*Pilgrim Hymnal* (Boston: The Pilgrim Press, 1931)
TPH	*The Presbyterian Hymnal* (Louisville, Ky.: Westminster/John Knox Press, 1989)
UMH	*The United Methodist Hymnal* (Nashville: Abingdon Press, 1989)
WB	*The Worshipbook* (Philadelphia: The Westminster Press, United Presbyterian Church [USA], 1970)

PART I

Women, Word, and Song

1

BIRTHING

(Advent)

INTRODUCTION

Two women, both pregnant, greet each other — and an instantaneous bond is formed between and deep within them, confirming their identities as bearers of life. In this astonishing moment of communion, each is strengthened in her calling.

This is the story of Mary and Elizabeth, but it is also the story of each of us. Truth always encompasses both the particular and the universal — which is why the ancient biblical account stirs such deep chords when women hear it.

In Luke's description of Mary's visit to Elizabeth, profound joy is predicated upon fear. The angel has just announced to the younger woman that she is to give birth; and she has accepted God's calling to a pregnancy out of wedlock, in ancient Judea a crime of adultery against one's betrothed. The punishment for such a sin, as Mary would have known, was death by stoning. This cultural background gives pointed meaning to the report that Mary "went with haste into the hill country. . . . " The image is not so much Christendom's traditional view of a young mother-to-be paying a visit to a beloved kinswoman but of a terrified, unmarried woman (perhaps, indeed, only a teenager) fleeing for her life to the temporary asylum of a "safe house" in the hills. The aged Elizabeth, the woman whom Mary seeks out for comfort, protection, and advice, is *herself* caught up in tenuous circumstances: well advanced in years and beyond the biological age of childbearing, Elizabeth must certainly have had her own collection of fears and hopes about her forthcoming delivery.

Both are women on the fringe of their society. The stirring words recalling their encounter and the spark of Life that it caused to leap within them weave a story of hope overcoming deathly fear. It is a reaffirmation of the importance of our mutual support, our community as women, in enabling us to continue bearing life into the world.

19

PREPARATION

In the publicity for this worship experience participants are invited to bring a Madonna and Child figure. The room is set up with four circles of six chairs each; and in the center of each circle is a low table, large enough to hold a candle as well as several Madonna and Child figures.

In the "Reading, Reflection, and Response" section two women offer insights about being women, being friends, and depending upon one another. The musical response, which provides transition, can be sung by a music leader *or* taped in advance. We suggest printing the words of the song "The Visit" to enhance the listening.[1]

•

CALL TO WORSHIP (unison)

Our souls are filled with wonder at the gift of our loving, and our spirits take on new meaning in the giving of love. God of the Flowing Well, you have looked upon us with favor as we join our lives in response to you.

Yes, from this time on all people who look upon us will recognize us as being life companions and will call us blessed; for you, the One who dwells in human hearts, have done great things for us.

Holy is your name, and your confirming joy reaches from age to age to those who dare to journey on the unknown pathways of committed love.

You have shown us the life-changing power of our love in the eyes of those who know us and in the richness of our work.

You have humbled us by the intensity of our otherness.

The false pride that we treasured in our ability to stand alone has been cast aside, and we understand ourselves and you more tenderly as we begin to experience the treasure of a lifetime of standing together.

We are no longer lonely: we touch with compassion those who come to us filled with needs.

You have opened the doors of eternity to us as we searched for you, mindful of your own longings for a people to love . . . according to the dreams and murmurings you have shared with those who love since the beginning of time . . . mindful of your own longings for a people to love, we recognize that the bondedness of human hearts and lives reflects one true reality of you, the Living God.

—Ann Johnson, *Miryam of Nazareth:*
Woman of Strength and Wisdom[2]

PRAYER OF CONFESSION

Unison: God our creator, who fashioned Eve after your own image, who blessed her and declared her good, hear my prayer.

Voice 1: Bless all women who labor to bring forth new life, who nurture the young, grant joy through their travail.

Voice 2: Bless all women who strive to become whole in new ways, who tread unstepped paths, grant fulfillment through their efforts.

Voice 3: Bless all women who create art, music, and literature, who open our eyes and lift our thoughts, grant new insight through their inspiration.

Unison: God our savior, who forgave the woman taken in adultery, who condemned not, but restored her to wholeness, hear my prayer.

Voice 4: Forgive all women who act out the violence in their lives, who strike back at the pain, grant them tranquility.

Voice 5: Forgive all women who are confined in prison cells, whose only crime may be poverty or desperation, grant them justice with mercy.

Voice 6: Forgive all women who debase their bodies, who seek pleasure or security at the price of their souls, grant them new lives of dignity.

Unison: God our comforter, who gave solace to Ruth and Naomi in their widowhood, who pitied Mary at the cross and sustained her, hear my prayer.

Voice 7: Comfort all women who are lonely, who are forgotten or afraid, grant them knowledge of your presence.

Voice 8: Comfort all women who are alone, again, through separation, divorce, desertion, or death, grant them new purpose and hope.

Voice 9: Comfort all women who are used or abused, whose rights are violated or denied, grant them peace.

Unison: O God, bless, forgive, and comfort me, for I am all women. Amen.

—Isobel Beaston[3]

ASSURANCE OF PARDON (singing)

I Was There to Hear Your Borning Cry[4]

I was there to hear your borning cry,
I'll be there when you are old.
I rejoiced the day you were baptized,
To see your life unfold.
I was there when you were but a child,
With a faith to suit you well;
In a blaze of light you wandered off
To find where demons dwell.

When you heard the wonder of the word
I was there to cheer you on;
You were raised to praise the living Lord,
To whom you now belong.
When you find someone to share your time
And you join your hearts as one,
I'll be there to make your verses rhyme
From dusk till rising sun.

In the middle ages of your life,
Not too old, nor longer young,
I'll be there to guide you through the night,
Complete what I've begun.
When the evening gently closes in
And you shut your weary eyes,
I'll be there as I have always been
With just one more surprise.

I'll be there to hear your borning cry,
I'll be there when you are old.
I rejoiced the day you were baptized,
To see your life unfold.

READING, REFLECTION, AND RESPONSE

Leader: Reads Luke 1:39–45 and offers reflection on the meaning
of Mary's journey to Elizabeth, as noted above on p. 19.

*Two participants present their thoughts about their fears as women, the need
for women to support one another, and their common experiences. When they
have finished proceed with the following:*

Leader: It is written that Mary said:

Unison: "My soul magnifies the sovereign and my spirit re-
joices in God my savior, who has regarded the low

estate of God's handmaiden. For behold, henceforth all generations will call me blessed." (Luke 1:46–48)

Leader: Today we express that differently:

My soul sees the land of freedom, my spirit will leave anxiety behind, the empty faces of women will be filled with life. We will become human beings long awaited by the generations sacrificed before us.

Reflecting: *Ten minutes in small groups.*

Leader: What are the fears from which you find yourself turning away?

Response: *Tape played: "O Mary, Don't You Weep" (verse 1).*[5]

Leader: It is written that Mary said:

Unison: "For the one who is mighty has done great things for me, and holy is God's name. And God's mercy is on those who fear God from generation to generation." (Luke 1:49–50)

Leader: Today we express that differently:

The great change that is taking place in us and through us will reach all — or it will not take place. Charity will come about when the oppressed can give up their wasted lives and learn to live themselves.

Reflecting: *Ten minutes in small groups.*

Leader: What does receiving mercy enable you to do?

Response: *Tape played: "O Mary, Don't You Weep" (verse 2).*

Leader: It is written that Mary said:

Unison: "God has shown strength with God's arm, and has scattered the proud in the imagination of their hearts. God has put down the mighty from their thrones, and exalted those of low degree." (Luke 1:51–52)

Leader: Today we express that differently:

We shall dispossess our owners and we shall laugh at those who claim to understand feminine nature. The rule of males over females will end. Objects will become subjects they will achieve their own better right.

Reflecting: *Ten minutes in small groups.*

Leader: When have you received strength from another woman?

Response: *Tape played: "O Mary, Don't You Weep" (verse 3).*

Leader: It is written that Mary said:

Unison: God has filled the hungry with good things, and has sent the rich empty away. God has helped God's servant Israel, in remembrance of God's mercy, as God spoke to our ancestors, to Abraham (and Sarah) and to their posterity for ever."

Leader: Today we express that differently:

Women will go to the moon and sit in parliaments. Their desire for self-determination will be fulfilled, the craving for power will go unheeded, their fears will be unnecessary and exploitation will come to an end

Reflecting: *Ten minutes in small groups.*

Leader: What is it that is coming to birth in you?

Response: *Tape played: "O Mary, Don't You Weep" (verse 4).*

Leader: *Reads Luke 1:56.*

— process by Gail A. Ricciuti and
Rosemary C. Mitchell; "Meditation
on Luke 1" by Dorothy Sölle[6]

LISTEN

"The Visit" (on tape), by Miriam Therese Winter

PRAYERS OF THE COMMUNITY

THE PEACE

During the peace, participants are invited to pass to each other the Madonna and child figures, saying "The peace of the Mother and Child be with you."

SONG

"Song of Mary," *The Presbyterian Hymnal*

BLESSING

SUGGESTED ALTERNATE HYMNS

"Born in the Night, Mary's Child" (TPH, WB)

"Come Thou Long Expected Jesus" (HB, PH, TPH, UMH, WB)

"O Mary, Don't You Weep" (UMH)

"The First One Ever" (UMH)

"To a Maid Engaged to Joseph" (TPH, UMH)

"What Child Is This?" (HB, PH, TPH, UMH, WB)

NOTES

1. "The Visit" is found in *WomanPrayer, WomanSong* by Miriam Therese Winter, Meyer-Stone Books, 1987. Available from Crossroad Publishing Co., New York.

2. Call to Worship reprinted from "Magnificat of Betrothal," *Miryam of Nazareth: Woman of Strength and Wisdom* by Ann Johnson, © 1984 by Ave Maria Press, Notre Dame, Ind. Used with permission of publisher.

3. The Prayer of Confession is by Isobel H. Beaston, Holmes, Pa., from the November 1987 *Concern Newsfold.* Used with permission.

4. "I Was There to Hear Your Borning Cry," words and music by John Ylvisaker. Used by permission. © 1985 John Ylvisaker, Box 321, Waverly, IA 50677.

5. "O Mary, Don't You Weep" (traditional) recorded by Holly Near, Pete Seeger, Ronnie Gilbert, and Arlo Guthrie on the album, HARP. © 1985 Redwood Records, 476 W. MacArthur Blvd., Oakland, CA 94609.

6. "Meditation on Luke 1" is adapted from *Revolutionary Patience*, by Dorothy Sölle as published by Orbis Books, Maryknoll, NY 10545. © 1977. Used with permission.

2

THE HOLY EMERGES FROM THE DARKNESS

(Advent)

INTRODUCTION

The symbols of darkness and light have always played an important role in expression of the most profound theological truths. Using that contrast, the faith community often speaks of the experiences of conversion and redemption and describes the struggle between good and evil. However, in emphasizing the polarity between light as good and darkness as evil, we have unwittingly robbed ourselves of the awareness that *darkness* can be a source of birth and blessing, a place where God waits to meet us. We have also been guilty of the sin of racism with an unexamined definition of light/white as "holy" and darkness/blackness as "sinister."

Advent, the season when our northern hemisphere moves deeper and deeper into shadow, is a time to reacquaint ourselves theologically with the blessed dark...and perhaps to re-enter our own dark places as we wait once more for Emmanuel to be born in us. What may initially seem frightful to us, as her pregnancy must surely have seemed to Mary (see above, p. 19), *can* be transformed to sacred space.

In her book *Godding*, Dr. Virginia Ramey Mollenkott reflects on "Godding in the Dark."[1] She recommends that we recover a positive theology of darkness, with its creative and healing significance, and thereby deepen our connection with the often-neglected right brain. It is this right side of the brain that directs the "feminine" or "dark" side of the body, according to the ancient theory of bodily "humors." Since the "masculine" elements were believed to be air and fire and the "feminine" elements earth and water, Mollenkott writes, "What a relief to realize that roots grow and thrive in *dirt*, in the moist cold darkness of the earth, and therefore suggest that God, the Ground of our Being and Becoming, is *darkness* as well as light!"

By honoring the darkness during this time of holy expectancy, we seek to nurture those roots that ultimately will yield the fruits of God's Spirit for ministry in the world.

PREPARATION

The room is set up with four or five small circles of chairs with small tables holding unlit candles around the room's perimeter. There should be at least as many unlit candles of varying sizes as the expected number of participants. A large Christ candle stands in the center of the room. The room should be as dark as possible, but with just enough light to allow participants to read. The opening of worship is spoken in complete darkness, with the leaders using small penlights to follow their parts.

•

WORDS TO GATHER US

Leader: Mary was a virtuous woman,
a woman of strength,
a woman who lived according to the rules of her time.
On a certain day
she heard the voice of an angel sent by God.

All: And the angel said:
"Hail, O favored one, the Lord is with you."

Leader: This greeting was odd and unfamiliar.
Mary was troubled,

Voice 1: Frightened

Voice 2: Anxious

Voice 3: Startled

Voice 4: Disturbed

Leader: And she thoughtfully pondered what it could mean.

All: And the angel said:
"Do not be afraid, Mary,
for you have found favor with God.
You will conceive in your womb,
you will bear a son,
you will call his name Jesus."

Leader: And the angel sang on about the greatness of her child.

Voice 1: But Mary was a woman who knew herself, and asked,
"How shall this be? I have no husband."

All: And the angel said:
        "The Holy Spirit will come upon you,
        the power of the most high will overshadow you,
        the child to be born will be called holy."

Leader: Out of the shadows.
           Out of the darkening experience of the overshadowing
           of God, will emerge what is Holy.

                                        — Rosemary C. Mitchell

All: Come, sweet darkness,
        come, enfold me,
        come, my mother,
        come and hold me,
        give me comfort,
        give me shelter,
        from the burning of the day.

                                        — Ken Medema[2]

SONG

"O Come, O Come, Emmanuel" (verses 1 and 2 only)

READING

[One] lesson to be learned was how to receive a blessing that caused
more problems than it solved.

"How can this be?" the words kept going through Mary's head as
she sat in her chambers....

Mary was poor and unmarried. And the angel's strange greeting
continued to haunt the young woman.

> "Hail, O Favored One! The Lord is with you!
> You are blessed among women!" (Luke 1:28)

At least Elizabeth was married. Still, Mary needed someone to talk
with. Someone who knew what it meant to grapple with God's inten-
tions. Someone. A Woman, pregnant like herself. Mary's mind kept
going back to the old woman Elizabeth. Suppose her kinswoman did
not believe her? It was a chance Mary had to take. She needed to talk
with another woman.

                                        — Renita Weems, *Just a Sister Away*[3]

SILENT PONDERING

LISTENING

Selections from "December" by George Winston[4]

MARY'S EXPERIENCE OF DARKNESS

Luke 1:39–45

READING

How might your life have been different if, as a young woman, there had been a place for you, a place where you could go to be among women...a place for you when you had feelings of darkness? And, if there had been another woman, somewhat older, to be with you in your darkness, to be with you until you spoke...spoke out your pain and anger and sorrow.

And if you had spoken until you had understood the sense of your feelings, how they reflected your own nature, your own deepest nature, crying out of the darkness, struggling to be heard.

And, what if, after that, every time you had feelings of darkness, you knew that the woman would come to be with you, and would sit quietly by as you went into your darkness to listen to your feelings and bring them to birth....So that, over the years, companioned by the woman, you learned to no longer fear your darkness, but to trust it...to trust it as the place where you could meet your own deepest nature and give it voice.

— Judith Duerk, *A Circle of Stones*[5]

REFLECTION (small group discussion)

- How would life be different if we welcomed the darkness?
- How shall we receive a blessing that causes more problems than it solves?

CELEBRATING: The Holy Emerges from the Dark

Each person is invited to light a taper from the Christ candle, then light another candle placed in the room. As you light a candle, stand facing it for a moment of silence, feel the light illumine your face, and give thanks for the darkness in you that makes space for the light to come.

SONG

"For Ages Women Hoped and Prayed," in Jane Parker Huber, *A Singing Faith*

MAGNIFICAT FOR TODAY

> *One:* Our souls magnify the holiness that dwells within us.
>
> *Two:* And our spirits rejoice in the presence of the Holy One.

Three: Because we as women have been touched and called.

All: Yes, from this day forward all generations will call us blessed.

One: For great things have been done through us and those who went before us.

Three: Holy is our name and we have shown mercy and strength as women, from age to age.

Two: We have gathered our courage and steadfastness and worked to heal the brokenhearted with tenderness and care.

One: Yes, we have been hungry and filled each other with good things.

Two: For we have kept our promises and journeyed and struggled, hope of our dreams...touching and healing ...laughing and crying...questioning and loving....

All: Yes, indeed, by our living and our faithfulness, by our passion and our courage...all generations of women from this day forth will be blessed.

—Diann Neu[6]

SONG

"O Come, O Come, Emmanuel" (verses 2 and 3 only)

BLESSING

One: In darkness as in light, may the Holy One seek and call us to bear Her life in the world.

All: In darkness as in light, may we hear, and bear, and bear each other up.

One: Blessing on you, my sisters.

All: Blessing on you, our sister. Amen, Amen.

—Gail A. Ricciuti

•

SUGGESTED ALTERNATE HYMNS

"Be Thou My Vision" (vs. 1, 2, 4) (HB, PH, TPH, UMH, WB)

"Blessed Jesus at Your Word" (PH, TPH, UMH, WB)

"Born in the Night, Mary's Child" (TPH, WB)

"Comfort, Comfort You My People" (vs. 1, 3) (PH, TPH, WB)

"Let All Mortal Flesh Keep Silence" (HB, PH, UMH, WB)

"O Day of God Draw Nigh" (PH, TPH, UMH, WB)

"People, Look East" (UMH)

"The Desert Shall Rejoice" (TPH)

NOTES

1. *Godding: Human Responsibility and the Bible* (New York: Crossroad, 1987), pp. 65ff.
2. "Come, Sweet Darkness" by Ken Medema from *Godding* by Virginia Mollenkott, © 1987. Crossroad/Continuum.
3. Excerpt reprinted from *Just a Sister Away: A Womanist Vision of Women's Relationships in the Bible* by Renita Weems. © 1988 by LuraMedia, San Diego, Calif. Used with permission.
4. "December," recorded by George Winston, Windham Hill Records (a division of Windham Hill Productions) © 1982, Stanford, CA 94305.
5. Reprinted from *A Circle of Stones: Woman's Journey to Herself* by Judith Duerk. © 1989. LuraMedia. San Diego, Calif. Used with permission.
6. "Magnificat for Today," by Diann Neu, co-director of (WATER) Women's Alliance for Theology, Ethics, and Ritual, 8035 13th Street, Silver Spring, MD 20910. Used by permission.

3

THE JOURNEY IS HOME
(Advent)

INTRODUCTION

The late Nelle Morton — social activist, educator, professor, theologian, reformer, woman of radical faith — remembered how powerfully she had been affected by a phrase in the feminist hymn "Lead On, O Cloud of Yahweh." The words "we are still God's people, the journey is our home" seemed to describe her own experience of journeying on unexpected paths, and even of being called to *construct* the road along the way. Pondering the meaning of "journey," she came to realize that "home was not a place [but] a movement, a quality of relationship, a state where people seek to be 'their own,' and increasingly responsible for the world."[1]

The wisdom of Nelle Morton's insight is liberating for many women who, feeling themselves sidetracked by the many demands of child rearing, family caretaking, and even their own "biological clocks," often joke about "what I want to be when I grow up!" This valuing of the journey itself is also theologically sound; for we believe, and counsel those seeking to join the church, that professing one's faith in Jesus Christ is indeed the *beginning* of a lifelong journey and not a sign that one has already "arrived."

In the same way, the metaphor of journey as "home" is appropriate to the Advent season — the beginning of the church's liturgical year and our spiral story of faith. It is here, on our way to Bethlehem, that we begin to discover who we are called to be and to understand more profoundly that we too — with Mary and with Nelle — are on the way to giving birth!

PREPARATION

The room is arranged in five semicircles of chairs. A small table in each semicircle is candlelit, with candlelight in the windows as well. The semicircles should all face the same direction so that participants can view the film and hold group discussions without rearranging chairs.

•

WORDS FOR REFLECTION
(printed, for meditation before worship)

We find our stories through the hallows of time;
through the corridors, halls, byways, and
sidewalks of history.
Our stories jump out at us;
taken by surprise
in
their locked up corners;
chained
to the walls of the past of men.

They leap to freedom — dancing —
hopping with joy — at being set free —
unchained — unlocked.
They leap into presence —
creating —
becoming —
the true (free) past and present of women.

We reclaim — see our stories —
through the cleansing (freeing)
mirror of women's history.

— Kathi Wolfe[2]

GATHERING WORDS

Leader: Life is a journey with others;
We travel as a people, on a winding road.
We share our lives,
   our experiences,
   our hopes,
   our fears.

People: With joy and hope we welcome other travelers
to share our lives.
We learn from each other.
We laugh and cry with each other.
We are at home with each other.

Leader: Life is a series of hellos and goodbyes.
There are those who arrive to be with us.
There are those who move ahead of us
beyond death.

People: Both in laying-hold and letting-go
we celebrate God's goodness.

We affirm the Spirit's presence
in the journey
in being home.

— Rosemary C. Mitchell, Gail A. Ricciuti

SONG

"It Came Upon a Midnight Clear,"
words from *Because We are One People*

FILM: *The Journey Is Home*[3]

Nelle Morton was born in 1905 in Sullivan County, Tennessee, and
worked as a public school art teacher in Kingsport, Tennessee, before
deciding to seek a "religious" career. She received her seminary education from the New York Theological Seminary and the University of
Geneva. In the 1940s, she became executive director of the interracial
Fellowship of Southern Churchmen. Later, her commitment to justice
for those marginalized in society continued when she accepted a post
teaching children with learning disabilities.

In 1956, Nelle Morton joined the theological faculty of Drew University in Madison, New Jersey, as professor of Christian Education.
It was at Drew that she became increasingly aware of the effects of
patriarchy upon the lives of minority groups, including women and
children, and the natural world; and it became her concern that religion often conspires to support patterns of patriarchal domination. She
became the first theologian to teach a university course on women, theology, and language, and is known as forerunner and mentor by many
contemporary feminist theologians. Nelle Morton died in July 1987,
but her prophetic vision will continue to be a beacon for women in
the church, and all persons who work passionately for human rights,
for years to come.

SCRIPTURE

Hebrews 11:1–14

REFLECTION: Mapping Our Journeys

*Provide each participant with a photocopy of a state map. Any state can be
used, but preferably one that has many place names with symbolic meanings.
The state of Washington, for example, has such places as "Port Gamble,"
"Discovery Bay," "Darrington," "Waitsburg," "Opportunity," "Tensed."
Participants are asked to study the map in silence, circling in red those
names that have particular meaning for their own metaphorical and spiritual journeys and starring the one name that is especially significant to*

*them. Then they are asked to complete the following questions, printed out
in their worship bulletin or on a separate sheet:*

- The capital of my life now is _____ .

- I'm being called by God to leave the following "country" (i.e.,
  what metaphorical place): _____ ; "kindred" (what group am I
  moving away from?): _____ ; "ancestral home" (what part of my
  heritage or past values?): _____ .

- My hunch is that the homeland I am seeking looks like this (list
  its characteristics): _____ .

- ...and its capital is _____ .

*After completing these questions in silence, participants gather in pairs or
small groups to share insights discovered through this process. Finally, the
whole group reconvenes to name aloud the capital of the homeland(s) they
are seeking.*

— process by Gail A. Ricciuti

SONG

Fruit and Seed
tune: "Greensleeves"

We are the fruit; we are the seed,
The past is spiraling through us.
What life will bloom, no one can tell,
The cycle keeps on moving.

Refrain:
This is our mothers' gift,
the cycle spiraling through us.
Thanks, thanks, to them we sing
and give it to our daughters.

Future and past are with us now,
We're moving on together.
We're gaining strength from her-story
The gift from mothers to daughters.

We are the old and we are new,
The future's spiraling onward.
The cycle bonds in sister love,
The future now we are making.

— Words: Sandra Amundsen,
Sing a WomanSong[4]

CLOSING PRAYER (unison)

We give you thanks,
Gentle One who has touched our soul.
You have loved us from the moment of our first awakening
and have held us in joy and in grief.
Stay with us we pray.
Grace us with your presence
and with it the fullness of our own humanity.
Help us claim our strength and need,
our awesomeness and fragile beauty,
that encouraged by the truth we might work
to restore compassion to the human family
and renew the face of the earth. Amen.

—Janet Schaffran and Pat Kozak,
More Than Words[5]

•

SUGGESTED ALTERNATE HYMNS

"All Beautiful the March of Days" (HB, TPH, WB)

"Be Thou My Vision" (HB, PH, TPH, UMH, WB)

"Break Forth O Living Light" (vs. 2, 4, 5) (WB)

"Come, O Thou Traveler Unknown" (UMH)

"God of Our Life through All the Circling Years (HB, PH, TPH, WB)

NOTES

1. Introduction, in Nelle Morton, *The Journey Is Home* (Boston: Beacon Press, 1985), p. xix.

2. Words for Reflection by Kathi Wolfe from *The Journey Is Home* by Nelle Morton. © 1985. Reprinted by permission of Beacon Press.

3. *The Journey Is Home* is available for rental or purchase from Ecufilm (800-251-4091).

4. "Fruit and Seed," words by Sandra Amundsen © 1974, from *Sing a WomanSong*.

5. The closing prayer is from *More Than Words* by Janet Schaffran and Pat Kozak. Meyer-Stone Books, 1988. Available from Crossroad Publishing Co., New York.

4

SOPHIA:
THE WISDOM OF GOD
(Epiphany)

INTRODUCTION

In both Jewish and Christian Scriptures, Wisdom is personified and given the power of divinity. She is *feminine* — *chokma* in Hebrew and *sophia* in Greek — but her identity varies. Wisdom sometimes appears to be a goddess-like figure, sometimes a child at play, sometimes an architect who collaborates with God.

Through the ages, Sophia's power as a feminine image was gradually repressed. Philo substituted the masculine "Logos" or "word" for Sophia. Although in Matthew Jesus speaks Sophia's words, and in John's Gospel his teachings use the style and symbolism of wisdom writings from the Hebrew Scriptures, the later church fathers abandoned references to Jesus as Sophia incarnate in an attempt to emphasize his equality to the *Father* God.

Yet Sophia as wisdom and as the heart of God's creative process appears throughout biblical writings. In the apocryphal book of Baruch (chapter 3), Sophia is hidden, and Yahweh searches for her. Only after Yahweh finds her does creation begin: an indication that Yahweh needed her to begin the divine creative process. She created the world *with* God in the Hebrew Scriptures, and was present in the ordering and re-creation of all things. John describes Jesus in these same terms at the opening of his Gospel — as existing with God in the beginning, the prerequisite for all other being: "Without him was not anything made that was made."

In the Genesis account, God creates from the outside — molding human beings from dust, separating the elements from each other. But the Scriptures show Wisdom to work in a more "feminine" manner. Wisdom pervades all things. She seeks communion. She renews the creation by changing the earth and human beings from within. "In

37

every generation she passes into holy souls and makes them friends of God, and prophets...."

In his New Testament epistles, Paul writes that the message of the crucifixion — that death leads to life — is perceived by the world as folly; but indeed, by God's action Jesus Christ has become our wisdom, our "sophia." The hidden Sophia of God, "which," he says, "we teach in our mysteries," is the Sophia that God predestined to be for our glory before the ages began. She is a Sophia that none of the masters of "this age" have ever known.

But Sophia is also a very *earthy* and earthly image, in contrast with much of the abstraction of Pauline theology. The writings we know as the book of Proverbs picture Wisdom as uniting the divine and the human: while She dances in God's presence, She also "delights to be among the [human race]." For Christians whose lives are centered in the everyday, connecting with this wisdom is a liberating relief.

In *Living in the Image of Christ*, Hans-Ruedi Weber points out that, while priests traditionally set down the prohibitions and permissions for moral life and the prophets authoritatively announced "Thus says the Lord!" the Israelite sages did not make decisions *for* those they counselled. Rather, they put forward alternatives — knowing that this world is a gray area where compromises cannot be avoided, where an entirely good or bad decision can seldom be reached.[1] The sages' teachings were aimed at leading people to maturity so that they could make responsible choices, as persons whom God trusts with the freedom to make wise *or* foolish decisions. Jesus, our Sophia, taught like a sage. Paradoxically, in modern cultures, which increasingly demand a clear dualism between good and bad, this mode of life is perceived as folly.

The identification of Jesus with Sophia, however, runs deeper than simply his way of teaching. Robert Lentz, whose life work is painting icons of contemporary and forgotten saints, has created an icon of "Christ Sophia."[2] She is a haloed woman bearing the prescribed Byzantine symbols for any icon representing the second person of the Trinity: Greek letters that stand for "I am who I am," and "Jesus Christ." In one raised hand she holds the ancient goddess statue "Venus of Willendorf"; and with the other hand, she points to herself. Lentz observes that this Christ Sophia is a dangerous memory for Christians. Certainly She has power to draw women disaffected with institutional Christianity *back* to their Christ!

PREPARATION

For this service participants are asked to bring a symbol of illumination to be placed on a table in a circle of chairs. (Five or six chairs compose each circle.) Candles also illumine each table.

Readings may be assigned to several people participating in the worship experience.

•

WORDS AND MUSIC FOR REFLECTION BEFORE WORSHIP

Come apart from the chaos awhile and dwell in the presence of God who is our source of being. God calls us to renew ourselves and our life's purpose and we gather with others who are searching. Let us be at prayer together.

Suggested Music: "Breaths," Sweet Honey in the Rock[3]

CALL TO WORSHIP

Leader: O Great Spirit!
whose breath gives life to the world
and whose voice is heard in the soft breeze,
we need your strength and wisdom.

People: May we walk in beauty.
May our eyes ever behold the red and purple sunset.

Leader: Make us wise so that we may understand
what you have taught us.

People: Help us learn the lessons you have hidden
in every leaf and rock.

Leader: Make us always ready to come to you
with clean hands and straight eyes.

People: So when life fades, as the fading sunset,
our spirits may come to you without shame.

—A Native American Prayer[4]

SONG

"For the Beauty of the Earth"; tune: Dix,
words from *Because We Are One People*

A TIME OF CONFESSION

Because the mystery of your being, Holy One, destroys our safe assumptions and shakes the foundations of our religiosity like a mighty earthquake,

Jesus Christ, Sophia, have mercy on us.

Because our hearts are unaccustomed to your intimacy with our lives,

Jesus Christ, Sophia, have mercy on us.

Because our heritage has been bound by our own acquiescence to a tradition that has limited you to maleness,

Jesus Christ, Sophia, have mercy on us.

Here there is a time of silent meditation. Worshippers are then invited to voice their own confessions, with each followed by the corporate response, "Jesus Christ, Sophia, have mercy on us."

—Gail A. Ricciuti

ASSURANCE OF PARDON

Christ, our Sophia, is not imprisoned by the limitations of our willingness or understanding. "In every generation She passes into holy souls and makes them friends of God...." And so, my sisters, I tell you the truth: In Her tender mercy is our liberation!

—Gail A. Ricciuti

SCRIPTURE, REFLECTIONS, RESPONSES ON SOPHIA: DIVINE WISDOM

The leader introduces the idea of Sophia as the Image of God. Resources for this section are listed on p. 43.

Sophia as Creator

> Scripture: Proverbs 8:27–31
> Wisdom of Solomon 7:25–27
> Ecclesiasticus 24:3–5

Reflections by Leader

Response (in small groups):

• What woman has been your source of wisdom?
  Each woman shares her response.

Sophia as Illumination

> Scripture: Proverbs 3:13–18
> Proverbs 4:5–9
> Ecclesiasticus 1:17–20

Reflections by Leader

Response (in small groups):

- What has been a source of illumination for you?
  Participants are encouraged to describe symbols they have brought.

Sophia as Christ: The World's Folly

Scripture: 1 Corinthians 1:18–25; 3:18–23

Reflections by Leader

Responses (in small groups):

- What "folly" from Christ's teaching has become your wisdom?

SONG

"Be Thou My Vision"; tune: Slane, words adapted by Ruth C. Duck, *Everflowing Streams*

PRAYER OF AFFIRMATION (unison)

Inhabit our hearts, God of history, as You once inhabited human flesh.

Be here among us with all of Your wisdom, all of Your power, all of Your mercy, all of Your love, that we might learn to be like God from our God who came to be like us.

Holy are You. Holy are we who are one with You forever. Amen.

— Miriam Therese Winter,
WomanPrayer, WomanSong

CLOSING SONG

"We Are Simply Asked," Jim Strathdee, in *Songs of Shalom*

BENEDICTION

Leader:	May you walk with God
All:	May you walk with God
Leader:	In the daily unfolding,
All:	In the daily unfolding,
Leader:	In the sharp pain of growing,
All:	In the sharp pain of growing,
Leader:	In the midst of confusion,
All:	In the midst of confusion,

Leader: In the bright light of knowing.

All: In the bright light of knowing.

Leader: May you live in God,

All: May you live in God,

Leader: In Her constant compassion,

All: In Her constant compassion,

Leader: May yours increase,

All: May yours increase,

Leader: In Her infinite wisdom,

All: In Her infinite wisdom,

Leader: In Her passion for peace.

All: In Her passion for peace.

Leader: May you walk with God

All: May you walk with God

Leader: And live in God

All: And live in God

Leader: And remain with God

All: And remain with God

Leader: Forever. Amen.

All: Forever. Amen.

— Miriam Therese Winter,
WomanPrayer, WomanSong[5]

MUSIC FOR REFLECTION

"Before I Even Spoke," by Carole Etzler,
in "Woman River Flowing On"[6]

•

SUGGESTED ALTERNATE HYMNS

"God of Grace, God of Glory" (HB, PH, TPH, UMH, WB)

"Holy Spirit, Truth Divine" (HB, PH, TPH, UMH, WB)

"Spirit Divine, Attend Our Prayers" (HB, PH, TPH, UMH, WB)

"Spirit of God, Descend Upon My Heart" (HB, PH, TPH, UMH, WB)

"Wellspring of Wisdom" (UMH)

RESOURCES FOR REFLECTIONS

Cady, Susan, Marian Ronan, and Hal Taussig. *Sophia*. San Francisco: Harper & Row, 1986.

————. *Wisdom's Feast: Sophia in Study and Celebration*. San Francisco: Harper & Row, 1989.

Mollenkott, Virginia Ramey. *The Divine Feminine*. New York: Crossroad, 1984.

Russell, Letty M. *Household of Freedom*. Philadelphia: Westminster Press, 1987.

Weber, Hans-Ruedi. *Living in the Image of Christ*. Valley Forge, Pa.: Judson Press, 1986.

NOTES

1. Hans-Ruedi Weber, *Living in the Image of Christ* (Valley Forge, Pa.: Judson Press, 1986).

2. We are indebted to Robert Lentz for insights about Christ Sophia, which inspired the Prayer of Confession and the Words of Assurance. His reflection upon his Christ Sophia icon appears in *Creation* 6, no. 4 (July/August 1990), published by Friends of Creation Spirituality, Inc., Oakland, Calif.

3. "Breaths," recorded by Sweet Honey in the Rock, Good News Album, Flying Fish Records, 1304 W. Schubert, Chicago, IL 60614.

4. The Call to Worship is from *In Accord: Let Us Worship* by Justo and Catherine Gonzalez, © 1981 by Friendship Press. Used by permission.

5. The Prayer of Affirmation and the Benediction are reprinted from *WomanPrayer, WomanSong* by Miriam Therese Winter, Meyer-Stone Books, 1987.

6. "Before I Even Spoke" words and music by Carole Etzler © 1977. "Woman River Flowing On" Album, 1978, Sisters Unlimited Inc., 1492 Willow Lake Dr., Atlanta, GA 30329.

5

THE WOMEN OF MARK

(Lent)

INTRODUCTION

Mark, with his usually sparse detail and somber tone, is sometimes overlooked as a source of women's "salvation history." It is *Luke's* Gospel that is more often favored by women seeking positive biblical metaphors for *our* lives in God's realm. Dr. Joanna Dewey, a New Testament scholar, suggested to the "Women, Word, and Song" community that we take another look at the richness of Mark with regard to women's role in Jesus' ministry.

The three women are nameless, as is so often the case in ancient writings; but it is Mark, of all the Gospel writers, who devotes most attention to the circumstances of their encounters with Jesus. The woman with the twelve-year flow of blood is given the dignity, in Mark's Gospel, of her own thoughts and feelings, and credited with all her attempts to regain wholeness. Only Matthew joins Mark in recounting the despair of the Syrophoenician woman whose little daughter was spirit-possessed. In Mark her quick-witted tenacity is noted by the Teacher, who commends her argument on the child's behalf by his response, "For this saying [Because of this word...] you may go your way; the demon has left your daughter." Again, Mark shares with Matthew the telling of Jesus' anointing at Bethany by a woman who extravagantly bathes his head with costly ointment: thoroughly detailing the story as if to honor the one whose devoted act "will be told in memory of her" wherever the Gospel is preached.

There is tremendous power in putting ourselves into such stories — going forth to meet this Jesus in the persons of our formerly unnamed sisters. Identifying with them places us in the tradition of the children of Sarah and Abraham, whose credo throughout the centuries has made the experience of the ancient Israelites their *own* history: "A wandering Aramean was my father; and he went down into Egypt and sojourned there, few in number; and there he became a nation, great, mighty, and populous. And the Egyptians treated us harshly, and afflicted us, and laid upon us hard bondage" (Deut. 26:5–6). The stories of faithful, tenacious, and courageous women must become *our* stories, thus literally re-membering them in a new and transforming way. One vehicle for giving flesh to this spiritual kinship is outlined in the worship experience below.

PREPARATION

To facilitate the cohesiveness of worship, the biblical passages should be printed in the bulletin. (We suggest using texts from *Mark as Story* by David Rhoads and Donald Michie, a clear and insightful translation of the Gospel.[1] Those we suggest for use appear at the end of this chapter.) Each passage should be numbered; a number 1, 2, or 3 also appears on the cover of each bulletin distributed before the service to facilitate the group process.

The room is arranged with chairs in groups of six; but after the Bible study the chairs are rearranged to form one large circle.

•

CALL TO WORSHIP

Leader: Gracious God, you show us the meaning of reconciliation in the life of Jesus Christ.

People: In his touch, his words, his actions, Jesus reconciled people to God and to the community.

Leader: We gather to renew ourselves that we too might reconcile others with a touch, a word, or an act.

People: We sing your praise, O God,
we proclaim your power to reconcile,
we pray for your realm to break in on our lives!

— Rosemary C. Mitchell

SONG

"Spirit," by Jim Manley in *Everflowing Streams*

SILENT TIME OF REFLECTION

WORDS OF ASSURANCE (unison)

O Holy Spirit,
Clear fountain,
In you we perceive God, how God gathers the perplexed and seeks the lost.

Bulwark of life,
you are the hope of oneness for that which is separate.
You are the girdle of propriety,
you are holy salvation.
Shelter those caught in evil,
free those in bondage,
for the divine power wills it.

You are the mighty way in which everything that is in the heavens,
on the earth, and under the earth,
is penetrated with connectedness,
is penetrated with relatedness. Amen.

—Hildegard of Bingen[2]

INTRODUCTION TO THE EVENING

The worship leader presents the theme for the worship experience.

THE WOMEN OF THE CRUCIFIXION

READING
Mark 15:25–16:8

REFLECTIONS BY THE COMMUNITY

SONG

We Find Thee, Lord
tune: Barbara Allen;
traditional folk melody;
author unknown

We find thee Lord in others' need,
In sisters and in brothers.
By loving word and kindly deed
We serve the One for others.

We look around and see thy face
Disfigured, marred, neglected.
We find thee Lord in every place.
Sought for and unexpected.

We offer in simplicity
Our loving gift and labor.
And what we do, we do to thee,
Incarnate in our neighbor.

We love since we are loved by thee.
New strength from thee we gather.
And in thy service we shall be
Made perfect with each other.

IDENTIFYING WITH THE WOMEN OF MARK

1. The Woman with the Flow of Blood
   Mark 5:24–34

2. The Syrophoenician Woman
   Mark 7:24–30

3. The Woman Anointing Jesus
   Mark 14:3–9

(passages printed at end of this service)

RESPONSE

Participants are asked to divide into groups of three according to the number found on their bulletin (see preparation above). In each group there is a person designated to be a 1, 2, and 3. The following process, also printed in the bulletin, is used:

a. Each person reads the biblical passage aloud to the others in the group. After all have read...

b. Each person tells the story without looking at the printed page. After all have told the story...

c. Each person again tells the story, but this time tells it in the first person. Each becomes the woman in the passage telling her own story.

d. After each person tells her story, the small groups answer this question:

   • "What do the women give to Jesus?"
   Participants are asked to write down their responses.[3]

LITANY (with sung response)

After answering the question in groups, participants form one large circle and share their answers. The answers form a litany with a sung response: a member of your community might be invited in advance to compose a simple text and melody, or you may use "Jesus Remember Me" from The Presbyterian Hymnal.

CLOSING

One: O Risen One, you gave your Word, saying:
        "You will be given power
        when the Holy Spirit comes upon you,
        and you will be my witnesses
        even to the ends of the earth."
        Come Spirit, now, we pray.

Unison: May the power of the Holy Spirit come upon us.
        May the wisdom of godly women encourage us.
        May the cloud of witnesses accompany us.
        And may we witness to the ends of the earth. Amen.

— Miriam Therese Winter,
WomanPrayer, WomanSong[4]

•

SUGGESTED ALTERNATE HYMNS

"Wind Who Makes All Winds That Blow" (TPH, UMH)

"Women in the Night" (UMH)

SUGGESTED PASSAGES TO BE USED FOR WORSHIP

1. The Woman with the Flow of Blood (Mark 5:24–34)

And Jesus went off with Jairus, and a huge crowd was following him and pressing him.

There was a woman who had a flow of blood over the course of twelve years and had suffered greatly under many doctors and spent everything she had and not been helped, but rather was getting worse. Hearing about Jesus, she came in the crowd from behind and touched his cloak, for she had been saying, "If I touch just his clothes, I'll be restored." And immediately the source of her bleeding withered up, and she knew in her body that she was cured of the ailment.

And Jesus, immediately aware in himself of the power that had gone out from him, turned around in the crowd and said, "Who touched my clothes?"

And his disciples said to him, "You're looking at the crowd pressing against you, and you say 'Who touched me?'" And Jesus kept looking around to see the one who had done this. Now the woman, frightened and trembling, having realized what had happened to her, came and fell before him and told him the whole truth. He said to her, "Daughter, your faith has restored you. Go off in peace and be free of your ailment."

2. The Syrophoenician Woman (Mark 7:24–30)

Now from there Jesus rose and went away to the territory of Tyre. And entering a house, he wanted no one to know about him, but he was not able to escape notice.

Instead, a woman whose little daughter had an unclean spirit immediately heard about him, came, and fell at his feet. Now the woman was Greek, a Syrophoenician by birth, yet she asked him to drive out the demon from her daughter.

And he said to her. "First let the children be satisfied, for it isn't right to take the bread for the children and throw it to the little dogs."

But she answered and said to him. "Lord, even the little dogs under the table eat the little children's crumbs."

And he said to her, "Because of this word, go off—the demon has gone out from your daughter." And going off to her house, she found the child thrown on the bed and the demon gone out.

3. The Woman Anointing Jesus (Mark 14:3–9)

Jesus was in Bethany, in the house of Simon the leper. While he was reclining to eat, a woman came who had an alabaster flask of very expensive pure nard ointment. Breaking open the alabaster flask she began pouring ointment on his head.

Now some were angry among themselves. "Why has this ointment been wasted? For this ointment could have been sold for over 300 denarii and the money given to the poor."

And they were harsh with her.

Jesus said, "Let her be. Why are you giving her trouble? It's a good work she did for me. For the poor you always have with you and whenever you want you're able to do good for them, but me you won't always have. What she was able to do, she did. She anointed my body ahead for the burial. I swear to you, wherever the good news is proclaimed in the whole world, what she did will also be told as a remembrance of her."

— trans. by David Rhoads and
Donald Michie, *Mark as Story*[5]

•

NOTES

1. David Rhoads and Donald Michie, *Mark as Story* (Minneapolis: Augsburg Press, 1982).

2. Permission to reprint excerpt from *Meditations with Hildegard* by Gabriele Uhlein, © 1983 by Bear & Company, Inc., has been granted by the publisher, Bear and Company, P.O. Drawer 2860, Santa Fe, NM 87504.

3. The process for the Bible study was developed by Donald Griggs, Griggs Educational Service, 638 Escondido Circle, Livermore, CA 94550. Used with permission.

4. The Closing words are reprinted from *WomanPrayer, WomanSong* by Miriam Therese Winter, Meyer-Stone Books, 1987.

5. Biblical passages are reprinted from *Mark as Story* by David Rhoads and Donald Michie. © 1982. Used by permission of Augsburg Press.

6

A WOMEN'S SERVICE
OF PENITENCE

(Lent)

INTRODUCTION

It is not a new discovery for feminists of faith, but one we have known
for long years: that not only are men the models of "righteousness"
in most traditional prayers, but even the examples of sinfulness are
male examples. Women so often have been denied an identity even
as *sinners*. The continuous translation that must happen in our heads
and hearts as we confess sins irrelevant to our experience as women
(and usually also in language that blatantly excludes us) is exhausting.
As theologian Valerie Saiving and others pointed out years ago, the
sins of pride and "will-to-power" are not temptations of which most
women are guilty; *we* should seek God's forgiveness for passivity and
underdevelopment or negation of the self.

With the invitation to self-examination offered by the Lenten season, we find ourselves hungering for an experience of confession and
forgiveness for which we have had no words or concepts. The soaring
hope of the psalmist's prayer "Restore unto me the joy of thy salvation"
can be ours only if the petition "Create in me a clean heart, O God"
genuinely expresses the content of our own lives as women who have
grown up in the milieu of patriarchy. Then shrivelled dreams can be
transformed freely into life-giving tears.

PREPARATION

The room is set with two large circles of chairs. In the center of each
circle is a low table on which are placed a candle, a basket of golden
raisins, and a chalice of water.

•

CALL TO WORSHIP

Now,
O Lord,
calm me into a quietness
   that heals
   and listens,
and molds my longings
and passions
   my wounds
      and wonderings
into a more holy
     and human shape.

—Ted Loder, *Guerrillas of Grace*[1]

SONG

"Holy Spirit, Truth Divine," from *The Presbyterian Hymnal*

LITANY OF PENITENCE (based on Psalm 51)

Unison: In your goodness, O God, have mercy on me;
with gentleness wipe away my faults;
cleanse me of guilt;
free me from my sins. (Ps. 51:1–2)

Voice 1:   There are men who deny the authority of women and limit their gifts. They lock away women's power, by trivializing them, ignoring them, abusing them.

Unison: We forgive those who sin against us.

Voice 2:   We ourselves undermine the authority of women. We limit the gifts of our selves. We lock away women's power and choose to hide our pain.

Unison: My faults are always before me;
my sins haunt my mind.
I sinned against you and no other,
knowing that my actions were wrong in your eyes.
But you love true sincerity,
so you teach me the depths of wisdom.

(Ps. 51:3, 4, 6,)

Voice 3:   Men fear those not like them. They have refused to acknowledge their weaknesses. They have locked away part of themselves.

Unison: We forgive those who sin against us.

Voice 4: Women have feared those who are like them; we have refused to know our strength. We have locked away part of ourselves.

Unison: Infuse me with joy and gladness.
Let these bones you have crushed dance for joy.
Create a pure heart in me, O God;
renew me with a steadfast spirit. (Ps. 51:8,10)

Voice 5: Men resist the Wisdom of God and refuse to seek her face.

Unison: We forgive those who sin against us.

Voice 6: We have denied that we are created in her image and hidden our knowledge of her.

Unison: Create a pure heart in me, O God.
Renew me with a steadfast Spirit. (Ps. 51:10)

— Rosemary C. Mitchell[2]

RITE OF ABSOLUTION

Leader: On the table is a basket of raisins. The raisins symbolize the dreams in our lives that have shrivelled and are in need of water. As the basket is passed you are invited to take a raisin from the basket and to reflect on the shrivelled dreams of your life.[3]

PRAYER

All: Gentle God who created us and directs our lives, Why is it that our dreams embarrass us? Why do we try to ignore them or consider them unimportant?

Is it too self-centered to work for our dreams? We seem threatened by our own self-esteem. The idea of self-worth frightens us. But in truth, we are free. The locks are sprung, the doors flung open. We can stand. We can walk. We are partners in creation. Amen.

— Janet Schaffran and Pat Kozak,
More Than Words[4]

PASSING OF THE BASKETS

The baskets are passed in silence. The leader then invites participants to spend a few minutes sharing their thoughts with each other.

Leader: On the table is also a chalice of water. As the chalice
            is passed from person to person, mark one another
            with the sign of a tear, saying: "May this sign of tears
            become for you God's life-giving water."

PRAYER

All: We give thanks to you, God, for sparkling water.
         For dreams that can be renewed,
         For lives replete with promise
         Pour over us this water of rebirth.
         Hover over us,
         as first your Spirit lingered over creation.
         Use the waters of creation;
         renew us, re-create us.
         May this water be your sign of life. Amen.

*The worship leaders begin the sign of tears in each circle. This is done by
each woman holding the chalice of water, dipping a finger into the water,
and marking her neighbor's cheek with a symbolic tear. The chalice is then
passed around the circle and each woman repeats this symbolic act until all
have received the sign of tears.*

PRAYER

All: God our Mother,
         You wash us
         and cleanse us
         and refresh us.
         In you we live and move and have our being.

Leader: "I will pour clean water upon you," says God, "and
            you shall be clean from all your uncleanness. From all
            your idols I will cleanse you. A fountain of life, a river
            of hope, in the desert of despair."

All: Wash away my guilt, O God, and cleanse me from my
         sin.

— Janet Schaffran and Pat Kozak,
More Than Words

*Following the prayer participants are invited to share their thoughts with
each other on what is becoming life-giving in them.*

SONG

"Amazing Grace" (traditional)

A WOMAN'S CREED (unison)

We believe in the goodness and value of women:
our strength and sanity;
our willingness to weep;
our capacity to support each other, instead of being rivals;
our ability to cope with children's demands and the burdens of life.

We have a willingness and ability to get on with the job; a spirituality and an earthiness, flowing with life, birth, death. We look forward to the future in faith and hope, working for the day when we and all our sisters are free to use all the gifts we have received and to share in all the benefits of human life and work.

We look forward to the age of peace, when violence is banished, when both women and men are able to love and to be loved. We believe that our future depends on us and that all the forces of good, love, peace, and justice, all the creative powers of the universe, work with us to achieve that vision.

May it come soon.

— Ann Wansbrough[5]

SONG

"God Speak to Me That I May Speak," words by Grace Moore, in *Everflowing Streams*

BLESSING

> *Leader:* May our loving Mother God water our dreams and bring us life. Amen.

•

SUGGESTED ALTERNATE HYMNS

"Behold the Lamb of God" (WB)

"Come Down, O Love Divine" (PH, TPH, UMH, WB)

"God of Compassion, In Mercy Befriend Us" (HB, WB)

"Pues Si Vivimos" (When We Are Living) (TPH, UMH)

"Take Thou Our Minds" (HB, TPH, WB)

NOTES

1. The Call to Worship is reprinted from *Guerrillas of Grace: Prayers for the Battle* by Ted Loder. © 1984. LuraMedia, Inc., San Diego, Calif. Used by permission.

2. The Litany of Penitence was adapted from a litany with the same title by Janet Morley in *All Desires Known*, published in the U.S. by Morehouse-Barlow Co., Inc. Used by permission of the author.

3. The Rite of Absolution is excerpted from *Women-Church* by Rosemary Radford Ruether. Copyright 1985 by Rosemary Radford Ruether. Reprinted by permission of HarperCollins Publishers.

4. The Prayers are from *More Than Words* by Janet Schaffran and Pat Kozak. Meyer-Stone Books, 1988.

5. "Women's Creed" by Rev. Ann Wansbrough, *Out of the Darkness*, Language and Liturgy Task Group, Commission on the Status of Women, Australian Council of Churches. © 1986. Used with permission.

7

WALKING HUMBLY WITH OUR GOD

(*Ordinary Time*)

INTRODUCTION

Sometimes the best way to express one's commitment and calling is not to tell it in words, but to dance it: when the medium for the message is to give it feet, legs, and arms! The prophet Micah knew this — or heard it from Yahweh with a mystic's ears; and so he wrote "this is what Yahweh asks of you: only this, to act . . . to love . . . to *walk*." None of these can be accomplished sitting passively. Our God asks for an expressive response to divine grace, not a theoretical one.

This is one of those times when worship that truly springs from the Word is incomplete without motion. In Judaism, the word for ethics is *halacha* — which also means "walking." And walking is accessible to *common* people, the ones who are not athletes, runners, discus throwers, skiers, long jumpers. (Some of us cannot walk well, so we limp, or hobble, or even roll along; but the idea is the same.)

It has been said that Jesus' most characteristic invitation was not "Believe!" but "Walk!" — that is, "Follow me»; and that was why his followers were not called Followers of Doctrine, but Followers of the Way. A "way" comes into view, ripens into reality, not merely by being hoped for but by being *walked*. The views are more precious, the oxygen in your lungs is palpable and delicious, and the engagement with others more demanding and more real when you have paced out long miles with your own two feet. This "walking the dusty road" theology is truly incarnational: to "walk humbly with your God" is also unavoidably to walk side by side with those who cry out for justice and who hunger to be loved.

Ethics, then, relates not to the "fancy stuff," but to walking — *halacha*. And walking, when all is said and done, is something no one else can do *for* you. In the words of the old spiritual, "You've got to

57

walk that lonesome valley, you have to walk it by yourself...." What we celebrate as Christian community is that we are called to walk the Way on our own two feet, together.

PREPARATION

For this service the setting should be a large meeting hall or church parlor, arranged with one large circle of chairs. For this celebration we invited women who had formed a sacred dance group in their church in a neighboring region. They offered to lead the worshippers in simple movements that blended with the theme.

The Music, Movement, and Reflection section is comprised of a familiar song, very simple movements, and reflections by three different women, which lead into the small group discussions to follow.

•

GATHERING WORDS

From the Hebrew Scriptures —
A New Translation of Psalm 23

God is our Mother, we shall not want.
She brings us rest, peace, and truth.
For the sake of justice in the world
She calls us forth to be liberators.

When we walk through anguished streets
cluttered with lies and brokenness,
we won't be afraid
because God is like us.

She holds us to her heart and breasts.
She comforts us.
She cares for us to care for each other.
She feeds us, loves us, heals us in the presence of the World.
Yes, for all to see.
God is good to us.
Our lives continue to overflow with her blessings.

God has called us to be truth-tellers.
We answer that call.
Goodness and mercy go with us each day of our lives.
We live in God's heart forever.

—Shelley A. Hamilton[1]

FROM THE HEBREW SCRIPTURES: A Prophetic Voice
Micah 6:6–8

MUSIC, MOVEMENT, AND REFLECTIONS

All sing: Spirit of the living God, fall afresh on me,
raise one arm out and up in front of you

Spirit of the living God, fall afresh on me,
raise the other arm out and up in front of you

Repeat

Melt me,
*arms in front, waist high, palms down, lower hands,
bending knees*

Mold me,
*slowly straighten legs, open fingers, work pretend ball
of clay*

Fill me,
form chalice with hands, raising arms

Use me,
continue up and open arms

Spirit of the living God, fall afresh on me.

Repeat beginning

Voice: Acting justly means...

Reflections by a planning team member

All sing (with movements):
Spirit of the living God, fall afresh on me,
Spirit of the living God, fall afresh on me,
Melt me, mold me, fill me, use me,
Spirit of the living God, fall afresh on me.

Voice: Loving tenderly means...

Reflections by planning team member

All sing (with movements):
Spirit of the living God, fall afresh on me,
Spirit of the living God, fall afresh on me,
Melt me, mold me, fill me, use me,
Spirit of the living God, fall afresh on me.

Voice: Walking humbly means...

Reflections by a planning team member

All sing (with movements):
Spirit of the living God, fall afresh on me,
Spirit of the living God, fall afresh on me,

Melt me, mold me, fill me, use me,
Spirit of the living God, fall afresh on me.

— "Spirit of the Living God";
words: Daniel Iverson[2]

UNISON PRAYER

O God, we are called
  to act justly,
  to love tenderly,
  to walk humbly with our God.
We hear those words as a call to partnership with you.
We know that to do as the prophet instructs means
  that we must change,
  that we must move,
  that we must get involved.
Make us strong enough, O God,
  to walk humbly so that we act justly
  and love tenderly each day;
So that we may grow to be strong people of faith,
  signs and symbols of new life. Amen.

— Rosemary C. Mitchell

SMALL GROUP REFLECTIONS
(in groups of three or four people)

• How do *you* hear the instruction of the prophet that we must "walk humbly with our God"?

A TIME TO LISTEN (recorded music)

"Take the Time," by Miriam Therese Winter,
in *WomanPrayer, WomanSong*[3]

LITANY OF AFFIRMATION

Leader: Anoint us to be a people of your Good News,
    yoked to break yokes,
    sighted to bring sight,
    healed to be healers,
    struggling to bring release.

People: Shower us and comfort us in the shining light
    and darkness of your glorious mystery.
    We invoke your mystery, not ours.
    We invoke your clarity, not ours.
    We invoke your truth, not ours.

Leader: Spirit of God,
            cry out through the cosmos, cry out through us.

People: Make your justice our work.
            Make your love real through our lives.

— Elizabeth Rice, *No Longer Strangers*[4]

SONG
repeat the words three times

God has given us the power to change our ways.
God has given us the power to change our ways.
Feed the hungry, loose the bound.
Walk humbly with our God.

— Mechtild of Magdeburg[5]

Music and movement for words are found in Creation Dances, *by Neil Douglas-Klotz.*[6]

CLOSING BLESSING

•

SUGGESTED ALTERNATE HYMNS

"Amazing Grace" (HB, TPH, UMH, WB)

"Blessed Jesus, at Your Word" (PH, TPH, UMH, WB)

"Come Down, O Love Divine" (PH, TPH, UMH, WB)

"From All That Dwell below the Skies" (HB, PH, TPH, UMH, WB)

"God of Compassion in Mercy Befriend Us" (HB, WB)

"Guide My Feet" (TPH)

"Jesus Walked This Lonesome Valley" (TPH)

"Sing with Hearts" (TPH)

"Spirit of God, Descend upon My Heart" (HB, PH, TPH, UMH, WB)

NOTES

1. A new translation of Psalm 23 is by Rev. Shelley A. Hamilton. Used with permission of author.
2. "Spirit of the Living God," authorized adaptation by Word of God, Ann Arbor, Mich. © 1935, 1963. Moody Bible Institute of Chicago. Used by permission.
3. "Take the Time," by Miriam Therese Winter, from *WomanPrayer, WomanSong*, Meyer-Stone Books, 1987.
4. Litany of Affirmation by Elizabeth Rice from *No Longer Strangers: A Resource for Women and Worship*, by Iben Gjerding and Katherine Kinnamon, 1983, World Council of Churches Publications, P.O. Box 2100, 1211 Geneva 2, Switzerland. Used with permission.
5. "God has given us the power to change our ways," words from *Meditations with Mechtild of Magdeburg*, published by Bear and Company, P.O. Drawer 2860, Santa Fe, NM 87504.
6. Music and movement from *Creation Dances*, by Neil Douglas-Klotz, Dances of Universal Peace, Peace Works, P.O. Box 626-C, Fairfax, CA 94930.

8

BLESSINGS

(Ordinary Time)

INTRODUCTION

The mode of worship and community that constitutes "Women, Word, and Song" gatherings is by its very nature richly rewarding but intensely demanding of participants, in a way that much of traditional Christian worship is not. Women who risk the freedom of expression, liberation of thought, and community relationship inherent in this approach experience — as Jesus promised — streams of living water welling up from within them, as a catalyst to spiritual journeying; and this (in a very positive sense) is hard work.

We have found ourselves growing increasingly sensitive to the necessity of rhythm in life: to the need for rest as well as intensity, drinking deep as well as drawing water up from the well, reflection as well as expression...in short, for *sabbaths* — even in the cycle of worship! So as summer approached to end the first year of this new worship experience, we felt moved to create a liturgy that would meet the community's need for respite at the end of a long winter's demands on overloaded lives. While most of our gatherings had offered an invitation for participants to wrestle with Scripture and to dialogue with one another, it seemed appropriate to make this service less demanding. A different sort of refreshment, in the form of benediction, was in order.

Jesus' Beatitudes are not only a challenge to radical discipleship but also proffer words of blessing on lives poured out to the limit: reminding us that healing and mercy, nurture and peace flow in reciprocal streams to refill healers, mercy-givers, nurturers, and peacemakers. In the months since the creation of this "Blessings" service, additional feminist resources have appeared that enrich this understanding of the Beatitudes. One is Christin Lore Weber's *Blessings: A WomanChrist Reflection on the Beatitudes*.[1] Another, of a different genre, is Alice Walker's 1989 novel *The Temple of My Familiar*, in which a chapter entitled "The Gospel according to Shug" re-visions and expands Jesus' blessings beginning with the words "Helped are they...."[2] And Neil Douglas-

Klotz plumbs new and ancient depths of these teachings, one by one, in *Prayers of the Cosmos: Meditations on the Aramaic Words of Jesus.*[3] Planners of future "blessing" gatherings will be blessed themselves by drawing upon the wisdom of such writers.

PREPARATION

For this relaxed gathering meant to be a symbolic "sigh of relief," chairs can be spaced in one large circle to lend airiness to the room. In the center a round table holds fruit, breads, and cheese arranged to be easily reached from any side.

•

CALL TO WORSHIP

Leader: God is my constant companion.

People: There is no need that God cannot fulfill.

Leader: When my pain is severe,
When my burden is heavy,
When my depression darkens my soul,
When I feel empty and alone,

People: God fills the aching vacuum.
I trust in God's promises.
God will not let me go.

— Rosemary C. Mitchell

DOXOLOGY

Praise God from whom all blessings flow,
Let songs rise up from earth below,
Let stars and galaxies enthrone.
Creator, Christ, and Spirit, One. Amen.

— words: David W. Romig;[4]
tune: Old Hundredth

RECEIVING THE BLESSINGS OF CHRIST: Matthew 5

Leader: Blessed are the poor in spirit, for theirs is the household of heaven.

All: How blessed are we who are needy in spirit or in flesh, whose lives are empty of all that really matters;

and a special blessing on those of us who seek to find our spirit, not by emptying ourselves, but by being filled up.

Leader: Blessed are all who mourn, for they shall be comforted.

All: How blessed are we who weep, who suffer unrecognized losses, who are not allowed to grieve, but are told to get on with our lives;

and a special blessing on those of us who begin to find joy where it never was before.

Leader: Blessed are the meek, for they shall inherit the earth.

All: How blessed are we who live and teach gentleness, who quietly draw out the gifts in those we encounter;

and a special blessing on those who struggle to develop self-respect, who no longer allow ourselves to be abused in the name of womanhood.

Leader: Blessed are all who hunger and thirst for righteousness, for they shall be satisfied.

All: How blessed are we who have been wronged, who long for a new age of justice to dawn;

and a special blessing on those of us who learn to act on our own behalf, rather than waiting to be taken care of.

Leader: Blessed are the merciful, for they shall be shown mercy.

All: How blessed are we who are ready to offer healing and forgiveness to those who are broken by their sins;

and a special blessing on those of us who are learning not to offer cheap grace by forgiving too easily.

Leader: Blessed are the pure in heart, for they shall see God.

All: How blessed are we who see things as they really are and call them by their right names with simplicity and grace;

and a special blessing on those of us who struggle to be wise as serpents without losing the innocence of our souls.

Leader: Blessed are the peacemakers, for they shall be called children of God.

All: How blessed are we who affirm the power of love, who choose life in a world of death, that our children might live;

and a special blessing on those of us who refuse to heal others' wounds lightly, who resist declaring peace when there is no peace.

Leader: Blessed are all who are persecuted for my sake, for their reward is great in heaven.

All: How blessed are we who endure suffering to bring God's world into new being;

and a special blessing on those of us who remember that Jesus did not call us to be victims as our way of life.

—Ann Evinger[5]

SONG

"Lady of Birth"; tune: "Lord of the Dance"; words: Ruth Duck, *Because We Are One People*

BECOMING A BLESSING

We suggest that participants simply repeat the unison parts after the leader to free their hands from holding a printed order of service.

Leader: We have received the blessing of Christ. We now take time to bless ourselves and one another. To embody our prayer, we use an old tradition, the laying on of hands.

Touch your eyes with your hands saying:

All: Bless my eyes that I may see clearly.

Leader: Touch your mouth saying:

All: Bless my mouth that I may break the silence of centuries and speak my truth.

Leader: Touch your ears saying:

All: Bless my ears that I may listen to the words, thoughts, and feelings of myself and each one.

Leader: Touch your heart saying:

All: Bless my heart that I may be open to friendship and love.

Leader: Touch your womb saying:

All: Bless my womb that I may be in touch with my creative energies of the universe.

Leader: Touch your feet saying:

All: Bless my feet that I may walk gently and go with courage on my journey.

Leader: Touch the person next to you saying:

All: Bless you, my friend.

Leader: Tonight we share blessings. We know that food alone is never enough for life. We need the nurture, nutrition, and sustenance that come from food that is shared, the enjoyment of one another's company, and the physical strength we derive from the food. We invite you to eat and to share the blessing of food and the blessing of company with friends.

—Diann Neu[6]

SHARING THE BLESSING WITH FRIENDS

At this time, all are invited to partake of the food and enjoy each other's company.

SONG

"We Plow the Fields"; tune: Dresden, *The Hymnbook*

CLOSING

Leader: "You will be given power when the Holy Spirit comes upon you, and you will be my witnesses even to the ends of the earth." Come, Spirit, now, we pray.

All: May the power of the Holy Spirit come upon us.
May the wisdom of godly women encourage us.
May the cloud of witnesses accompany us,
and may we witness to the ends of the earth. Amen.

—Miriam Therese Winter,
WomanPrayer, WomanSong[7]

•

SUGGESTED ALTERNATE HYMNS

"Become to Us the Living Bread" (TPH, WB)

"Bless the Lord, O My Soul" (TPH, WB)

"Come Thou Thankful People Come" (HB, PH, TPH, WB)

"For the Beauty of the Earth" (HB, PH, TPH, UMH, WB)

"God, Who Stretched the Spangled Heavens" (TPH, UMH)

"I've Got Peace Like a River" (TPH)

"Love Divine All Loves Excelling" (HB, PH, TPH, UMH, WB)

"What Gift Can We Bring?" (UMH)

NOTES

1. Christin Lore Weber, *Blessings: A WomanChrist Reflection on the Beatitudes* (San Francisco: Harper & Row, 1989).

2. Alice Walker, *The Temple of My Familiar* (New York: Simon and Schuster, 1989).

3. Neil Douglas-Klotz, *Prayers of the Cosmos: Meditations on the Aramaic Words of Jesus* (San Francisco: Harper & Row, 1990).

4. David W. Romig. Used with permission.

5. Ann Evinger. Used with permission.

6. The litany *Becoming a Blessing* by Diann Neu, co-director of WATER (Women's Alliance for Theology, Ethics and Ritual), 8035 13th Street, Suite 3, Silver Spring, MD 20910. Used by permission.

7. The Closing is by Miriam Therese Winter and is taken from her *WomanPrayer, WomanSong*, Meyer-Stone Books, 1987.

9

THE DISMISSED WOMAN

The Banishing of Queen Vashti (Ordinary Time)

INTRODUCTION

"Vashti was the beautiful queen of Xerxes, king of Persia. He was the most powerful monarch in the world: his kingdom stretched from India to Ethiopia. Vashti lived in a palace with marble pillars, slept in a bed inlaid with silver, and drank from a golden goblet.

"Xerxes held a great feast for all the governors of his provinces. He bragged about the beauty of his queen and then sent for her that he might display her to his guests. She refused to come.

"Humiliated before his officials, Xerxes asked his wise men what to do about his disobedient queen. They pointed out that the word would spread quickly to women all over the empire, and they would be tempted to disobey *their* husbands. The wise men told him to get rid of Vashti and to publish a law that women must be subject to their husbands."[1]

Renita Weems in her book *Just a Sister Away* gives us a womanist view of this story, recounting the story from a woman's perspective.[2] In a very powerful way, Dr. Weems uncovers for us the bond of women throughout the ages, the link we do indeed have with one another: for who we are is linked to who they were. This worship experience celebrates the strength and bondedness of women.

PREPARATION

The room arrangement for this service includes a pedestal in the center of the worship space, holding a large doll dressed in an elegant gown. Worshippers gather around tables that hold materials for making crowns: strips of bright paper, scissors, tape, stars, and glitter.

•

69

GATHERING WORDS

    Leader: Centuries of women are our sisters.

  Community: And we celebrate the lives they have lived.

    Leader: We hold up half the sky.

  Community: And we see its beauty stretched out before us.

    Leader: We have discovered the Divine within us, around us, and among us.

  Community: Let us celebrate this day and all that is before us.

                                      —World YWCA[3]

SONG

"We Gather Together" (verse 1 only), words adapted by Ruth Duck, *Everflowing Streams*

THE PEDESTAL EXPERIENCE

Participants are invited to create crowns for themselves (allow twenty minutes for this process). While they "create," the topic of conversation around the work tables is:

- In what ways does our culture still keep women on pedestals?

THE STORY OF QUEEN VASHTI

Esther 1:1–22

- What do you think of what Queen Vashti did?

THE VALOR OF VASHTI

  Reader 1:   What else was Vashti the Queen supposed to wear
besides her jeweled turban when the king
called for her prompt appearance at the banquet
where he was celebrating his success
in sovereignty and splendor? Must she dance
in sensuous rhythms to excite the fancies
of princes, nobles, governors, and generals
who had been dining and wining seven days and
    nights?

             When the seven trusted eunuch chamberlains
delivered the order, Vashti was not willing
and said so with a chaste and quiet candor.
Xerxes was baffled by her brash defiance
and asked his wise men how to bridge the impasse.

Reader 2:   Memucan summarized their august views
          by pointing out the plight, predicament,
          and pretty pass that all men of the kingdom
          would come to if their wives should ever learn
          of the queen's behavior

Voice 1:   of her obstinacy

Voice 2:   and her extreme unmanageability

Voice 3:   and having a mind of her own

Voice 4:   and using it.

Reader 2:   If he should treat her like a gentleman,
          he would be opening a Pandora's box
          of contempt and of wrath and willfulness,
          which might result in women's liberation!

Reader 1:   So they counseled him for all their sakes
          as well as his to muzzle the madcap queen
          and find another at his earliest
          convenience. Thereupon Ahasuerus
          (Xerxes' longer name) was pleased to oblige
          and sent a solemn letter in the language
          and script of every royal province
          saying each man in his own house was lord

Voice 1:   and master,

Voice 2:   boss,

Voice 3:   cock of the roost,

Voice 4:   and any other unpretentious titles

Reader 1:   that he might choose to fit his masculine
          modesty and manifest superiority.

All: Queen Vashti lost her crown but not her head.
          Xerxes had power to vacate her throne
          but not the knack to make her hate herself
          or denigrate her beautiful integrity.
          He could not terminate her majesty.

—Thomas John Carlisle,
Eve and After, adapted by the authors for this use[4]

GIVING UP OUR CROWNS

At this time each participant is invited to "give up her crown" by placing it at the base of the central pedestal.

> "I will no longer" [*each woman fills in the blank*].
> "You can have your crown back!"

THE WISDOM OF ESTHER

Esther 2:1–18

READING

It is not insignificant that it is through Queen Esther's memoirs that we even hear of the courageous queen by the name of Vashti. If Queen Esther had chosen to ignore the memory of the woman who preceded her on the throne, Queen Vashti might have been lost to history. (It was certainly unlikely that King Ahasuerus would have mentioned his first wife and her disgraceful behavior in his memoirs!)

But the king's second wife, Esther, had much for which to thank Vashti. King Ahasuerus might not have been so predisposed to forgive Queen Esther her brazen disobedience had not his first wife taught him that, like it or not, some women will make their own decisions. At least with Esther, the king was willing to hear her out.

By including Queen Vashti's story in her memoirs, Queen Esther set a precedent that we, like she, have a responsibility to our fallen leadership.

We have a responsibility to remember, celebrate, and come to the aid of those women who once gave of themselves on our behalf, but who for whatever reason — be it divorce, death of husband, or political defeat — now no longer occupy positions of leadership. We cannot afford to forget or trample on our feminine leaders of the past.

As sisters, it is our responsibility to remember the women, both single and married, who have worked to clear and pave the way for us, at the risk of health, sanity, comfort, reputation, family, and marriage.

If truth be told, we today are who we are — if we are anybody — because some woman, somewhere, stooped down long enough that we might climb on her back and ride piggyback into the future.

—Renita Weems, *Just a Sister Away*[5]

A LITANY OF TRUTH

Leader: We are called by Christ.
            We come to affirm our life in Christ.
            We come to dispel myths and lies,

to question and challenge injustice,
to question structures we know oppress women,
and hold us hostage.

Voice 1: It is not true that women should feel and experience that being a woman is of secondary value to the community.

All: It is true that women are created women, the image of God, co-workers with God in caring for life, in struggling for the liberation of humanity and for a world order that respects each one's dignity.

Voice 2: It is not true that women should accept rape, incest, battering, or any humiliation as the fate of women.

All: It is true that Christ has come into the world to heal the broken community between women and men, to restore our sense of self, dignity, and inclusion.

Voice 3: It is not true that young girls should be denied the opportunity to learn how to read, to write, and to analyze the developments of their country.

All: It is true that everyone is called to respond to the gift of life and to the needs of our community with all our heart, all our soul, and all our reason.

Voice 4: It is not true that sexual slavery, bondage, and prostitution are impossible to counteract and eliminate.

All: It is true that Christ has come into the world to overturn the tables of injustices. Women and men, empowered by the Holy Spirit, should challenge poverty and patriarchal culture.

And it is true that God the creator has given us the responsibility and trust to care for all of creation in humility and faithfulness, to work and to love as co-creators of God.

—Anna Karin Hammer, Jean Sindab[6]

BLESSING

Leader: May we, like Vashti,
be filled with majesty and integrity.
May we, like Esther,
remember our strong mothers of faith
And may we each be crowned
with the blessings of God.

Response: "We Gather Together" (verses 2 and 3),
          from *Everflowing Streams*

•

SUGGESTED ALTERNATE HYMNS

"God Created Heaven and Earth" (TPH, UMH)

NOTES

1. Introductory words by Betty Hemphill from *Third Testament Women* published by Lydian Press. 1979.

2. Renita Weems, *Just a Sister Away: A Womanist Vision of Women's Relationships in the Bible* (San Diego, Calif.: LuraMedia, 1988).

3. Gathering words used by permission of World YWCA, 37, Quai Wilson, 1201 Geneva, Switzerland.

4. "The Valor of Vashti" from *Eve and After* by Thomas John Carlisle. William B. Eerdmans Publishing Co., Grand Rapids, MI 49503. © 1984. Used by permission of the publisher.

5. Excerpt reprinted from *Just a Sister Away: A Womanist Vision of Women's Relationships in the Bible* by Renita Weems. © 1988 by LuraMedia, San Diego, Calif. Used by permission.

6. "Litany of Truth," by Anna Karin Hammer and Jean Sindab, from *Prayers and Poems — Songs and Stories*, Ecumenical Decade 1988–1998, "Churches in Solidarity with Women," 1988, World Council of Churches Publications, P.O. Box 2100, 1211 Geneva 2, Switzerland.

10

PROPHETIC VOICES
(World Communion Sunday)

INTRODUCTION

Prophecy in the Bible is not concerned primarily with the foretelling or predicting of future events the way a weather forecaster announces an impending storm. While *The American Heritage Dictionary of the English Language* (1982) and other such volumes rely heavily on emphasizing *prediction* as the function of the prophet, biblical prophecy deals rather with proclaiming the intuitively felt will of God in a specific moment and circumstance.

Because the repeated teaching of the prophets was that tomorrow is inherent in the implications of *these* times (a nuance that people of faith often indeed misconstrue as "prediction"), it is accurate to say that a prophet is one who imagines a new heaven and a new earth while being firmly rooted in this world. That is why "prophetic imagination" is so challenging and threatening to the powers-that-be.

Given women's socialization in a patriarchal culture, many of us have an experiential kinship with the Hebrew prophets — most of whom evidently did not *feel* equipped to be prophets when thrust by God into that role. As Dr. Carol Gilligan's research has found, many of us who are white, middle-class women in this society (recognizing that the life experience of women of color is quite different) somehow lost in early puberty the exquisite sense of self, and the valuing of our own ideas and dreams, that we possessed as little girls.[1] We need a new confidence to trust the prophetic within us. The ancient prophets, therefore, can serve as "spirit guides" for modern women seeking to discover, reclaim, and utilize our deepest intuitive springs.

PREPARATION

Participants are asked to bring a prophetic sign/symbol to be placed on a central table. The room is set up in a large circle, with a table in the center holding a tray of bread. A worship leader begins with words of introduction on the theme for the evening. As the litany "Blessing the Bread" is read, the worship leaders break the bread and pass it around the circle, inviting participants to take a piece of bread and to eat.

•

BLESSING THE BREAD: A Litany for Four Voices

The following text is not printed in the bulletin, but given only to the four readers; so that others will experience the effect of simply listening to the expressiveness of voices.

Voice 1:   In the beginning was God

Voice 2:   In the beginning, the source of all that is

Voice 3:   In the beginning, God yearning

Voice 4:   God, moaning

Voice 1:   God, laboring

Voice 2:   God, giving birth

Voice 3:   God, rejoicing

Voice 4:   And God loved what she had made

Voice 1:   And God said, "It is good."

Voice 2:   Then God, knowing that all that is good is shared

Voice 3:   Held the earth tenderly in her arms

Voice 4:   God yearned for relationship

Voice 1:   God longed to share the good earth

Voice 2:   And humanity was born in the yearning of God

Voice 3:   We were born to share the earth

Voice 4:   In the earth was the seed

Voice 1:   In the seed was the grain

Voice 2:   In the grain was the harvest

Voice 3:   In the harvest was the bread

Voice 4:   In the bread was the power

Voice 1:   And God said, All shall eat of the earth

Voice 2:   All shall eat of the seed

Voice 3: All shall eat of the grain

Voice 4: All shall eat of the harvest

Voice 1: All shall eat of the bread

Voice 2: All shall eat of the power

Voice 3: God said, You are my people

Voice 4: My friends

Voice 1: My lovers

Voice 2: My sisters

Voice 3: And brothers

Voice 4: All of you shall eat

Voice 1: Of the bread

Voice 2: And the power

Voice 3: All shall eat

Voice 4: Then God, gathering up her courage in love, said,

Voice 1: Let there be bread!

Voice 2: And God's sisters, her friends and lovers knelt on the earth

Voice 3: Planted the seeds

Voice 4: Prayed for the rain

Voice 1: Sang for the grain

Voice 2: Made the harvest

Voice 3: Cracked the wheat

Voice 4: Pounded the corn

Voice 1: Kneaded the dough

Voice 2: Kindled the fire

Voice 3: Filled the air with the smell of fresh bread

Voice 4: And there was bread!

Voice 1: And it was good!

Voice 2: We, the sisters of God say today

Voice 3: All shall eat of the bread

Voice 4: And the power,

Voice 1: We say today,

Voice 2:   All shall have power

Voice 3:   And bread.

Voice 4:   Today we say

Voice 1:   Let there be bread.

Voice 2:   By the power of GOD

Voice 3:   Women are blessed

Voice 4:   By the women of God

Voice 1:   The bread is blessed

Voice 2:   By the bread of God

Voice 3:   The power is blessed

Voice 4:   By the power of bread

Voice 1:   The power of women

Voice 2:   The power of God

Voice 3:   The people are blessed

Voices 1, 2, 3, 4:

              The earth is blessed
              The bread is rising.

                    — Carter Heyward, *Our Passion for Justice*[2]

SONG

"God Is Coming in the Form of My Sisters," Ruth C. Duck,
Sing a WomanSong[3]

WHAT IS, AND WHO IS, A PROPHET? Proverbs 31:10–31

Voice 1:   Who shall find a valiant woman?

Voice 2:   Who shall find a woman of strength?

Voice 1:   A pearl of great price is she.

Voice 2:   Her associates all have confidence in her and benefit from her expertise.

Voice 1:   She initiates good, not evil, every day of her life.

Voice 2:   She does not neglect her household tasks, she willingly works with her hands.

Voice 1:   Broadminded, her global perspective is a source of nurture for her.

Voice 2: She rises early, before the dawn, to prepare food for her family and organize the tasks of the day.

Voice 1: She considers her options, then makes her move, investing the experience she already has or even profits previously earned.

Voice 2: She works diligently, taking pride in her inner resources and strengths.

Voice 1: When her gifts are encouraged and their value affirmed, she will work well into the night, entering wholeheartedly into even the menial tasks.

Voice 2: She opens her heart to the needy, she is generous with the poor, yet she does not neglect her family's needs nor priorities of her own.

Voice 1: She is known for her dignity and strength, and she laughs at the days to come.

Voice 2: She often speaks with wisdom, and she teaches in a kindly way.

Voice 1: Those who are close to her praise her, her family and associates and friends: "Many women succeed or do outstanding things, but you surpass them all!"

Voice 2: Charm is superficial, and beauty fades, but the woman who is wise is the one to be praised.

Voice 1: May the public sector value her work, and may all applaud her integrity.

— Miriam Therese Winter,
WomanPrayer, WomanSong[4]

PROPHETIC SIGNS IN OUR LIVES

Participants are asked to go to the center table one by one, and to pick up their prophetic symbol. They are then invited to say their name and indicate why this symbol is prophetic for them. The worship leader may offer a brief meditation on the meaning of the word "prophetic" as it has been defined by these statements.

PRAYERS OF THANKSGIVING FOR PROPHETS IN OUR LIVES

During this time the participants are invited to call out the name of a woman, living or dead, whom they consider a prophet. After each name, worshippers respond:

> We praise valiant women,
> whose lives give us hope.

READING: "Write Your Own Bible"

I've been going there on retreat each year for the past forty years. Each time it's the same, yet somehow always different. The first time I went I forgot to bring my Bible. When I asked the guestmaster if I could borrow a Bible, he said, "Wouldn't you care to write your own?" "What do you mean?" "Well, write your own Bible — something of your own on the order of the Bible. You could tell of a classical bondage and the great liberation, a promised land, sacred songs, a messiah — that kind of thing. Ought to be much more interesting than just reading someone else's Bible. And you might learn more." Well, I set to work. It took me a month. I never learned so much about the official Bible. When I was finished, he recommended I take it home and try to live according to it for a year. I should keep a journal of my experience. But I shouldn't tell anybody about the project, nor show anyone the books. Next year, after Christmas I could come back for another retreat.

It was quite a year. An eyeopener. Most certainly I had never put so much energy and alertness into living by the official Bible as I was putting into living by this one. And my daily meditations had never been so concentrated.

When I arrived back for my next retreat, he greeted me very warmly, took into his hands my Bible and my journal, kissed them with greatest reverence, and told me I could now spend a couple days and nights in the Hall of the Great Fire. On the last night of the year, I should consign my two books to the flames. And that's what I did. A whole year's wisdom and labor — into the Great Fire. Afterwards he set me to work writing another Bible.

And so it went, these past forty years. Each year a new Bible, a new journal, and then at the end of the year — into the flames. Until now I have never told anyone about this.

—Theophane the Monk,
Tales of a Magic Monastery[5]

AN AFFIRMATION OF OUR OWN
PROPHETIC VOICES

After the reading participants are asked to divide into groups of two or three. In these groups they are invited to share their own words of prophecy: in other words to write their own Bible — to share the wisdom sparking their hearts about life and faith.

SONG

"One by One," by Miriam Therese Winter,
in *WomanPrayer, WomanSong*

READING

The prophet does not ask if the vision can be implemented, for questions of implementation are of no consequence until the vision can be imagined. The imagination must come before the implementation. Our culture is competent to implement almost anything and to imagine almost nothing. The same royal consciousness that makes it possible to implement anything and everything is the one that shrinks imagination because imagination is a danger. Thus every totalitarian regime is frightened of the artist. It is the vocation of the prophet to keep alive the ministry of imagination, to keep on conjuring and proposing alternative futures to the single one the king wants to urge as the only thinkable one.

— Walter Brueggemann,
The Prophetic Imagination[6]

Participants are invited once again to share the bread. All hold the bread as the blessing is read; then all eat together.

BLESSING (unison)

We, the sisters of God, say today
All shall eat of the bread,
And the power,
We say today,
All shall have power
And bread
Today we say
Let there be bread.
And let there be power!
Let us eat of the bread and the power!
And all will be filled
For the bread is rising!
By the power of God
Women are blessed.
By the women of God
The bread is blessed.
By the bread of God
The power is blessed.
By the power of bread
The power of women
The power of God

The people are blessed,
The earth is blessed
And the bread is rising. Amen.

—Carter Heyward[7]

•

SUGGESTED ALTERNATE HYMNS

"All Who Love and Serve Your City" (vs. 1, 2, 3, 5,) (TPH, UMH, WB)

"Be Thou My Vision" (vs. 1, 2, 4) (HB, PH, TPH, UMH, WB)

"Eternal God Whose Power Upholds" (HB, PH, TPH, WB)

"For the Bread Which You Have Broken" (HB, TPH, UMH)

"God Gives the People Strength" (WB)

"God of the Ages by Whose Hand" (WB)

"Let There Be Light" (vs. 1, 2, 4) (HB, PH, UMH, WB)

"Though I May Speak" (TPH, UMH)

NOTES

1. Carol Gilligan, Nona P. Lyons, Trudy J. Hamner, eds., *Making Connections: The Relational Worlds of Adolescent Girls at Emma Willard School* (Cambridge, Mass.: Harvard University Press, 1990).

2. "Blessing the Bread." Used by permission from the publisher of *Our Passion for Justice: Images of Power, Sexuality and Liberation* by Carter Heyward, Pilgrim Press, New York. © 1984.

3. "God Is Coming in the Form of My Sisters," words and music by Ruth Duck, from *Sing a WomanSong*, The Ecumenical Women's Center, Chicago. 1975.

4. The paraphrases of Proverbs 31 and "One by One" are reprinted from *WomanPrayer, WomanSong*, by Miriam Therese Winter, Meyer-Stone Books, 1987.

5. Theophane the Monk, *Tales of a Magic Monastery* (New York: Crossroad, 1981).

6. Excerpt reprinted from *The Prophetic Imagination* by Walter Brueggemann. © 1978. Used by permission of Augsburg Press.

7. Carter Heyward, "Blessing the Bread."

11

WEAVERS OF THE WEB
(Ordinary Time/Summer Solstice)

INTRODUCTION

"...that they may be one even as we are one, I in them and thou in me, that they may become perfectly one...." This prayer of Jesus, which is so often called his "high-priestly prayer," is also strikingly a *weaver's* prayer, whereby this artisan of the spirit ravels the threads of our lives together in, and with, God. If one explores the text from the standpoint of rhetorical criticism (the model used by Dr. Phyllis Trible in her books *God and the Rhetoric of Sexuality* and *Texts of Terror*), the interweaving of Jesus' words and the convolution of the text suggest the pattern of a mandala or a web — something more intricate, even, than warp and woof.

The web of creation is spun and woven by the great Mother — Spiderwoman, our native forebears named her — bringing into being all life out of the stuff of Herself. The memory of our grandmothers darning their family's socks late into the night evokes strands of that other, ancient, memory. Even the modern science of genetics triggers a sacred recognition, like the vibration of a cosmic web, with computer-imaged threads of DNA being knit into Life.

There is something women by nature understand about the deep significance of all web images, which confirm in us the truth that in God, with God, and with the earth we all indeed are one.

PREPARATION

With this theme in mind, movement and even music for worship are structured in such a way that "web" patterns are suggested. The prelude music and melodies sung by participants are chants and rounds — so that the singing will swirl and interweave the worship space. Accompaniment to the singing of rounds can be hauntingly beautiful if played by two or three flutists, without additional background.

The worship space is arranged in a large circle, to accommodate "weaving of the web" during response to the readings. The text from the Gospel of John should be printed as a unison reading, although we have omitted it here. Other materials needed for use in the service are several pairs of scissors and a large ball of deep red yarn.

If possible, the worship space should be framed either by clotheslines on which medium-weight fabric pieces can be hung, or by vertical wooden standards with long crossbars for the same purpose. Participants are requested to bring with them a flat piece such as an afghan, shawl, tablecloth, runner, or wall hanging that has been woven, knitted, crocheted, or knotted. These are hung around the room as people enter the worship space, thereby creating an environment for the service.

•

PRELUDE

"A Circle Is Cast" by Libana[1]

REFLECTION BEFORE WORSHIP: The Web

As I walked through the woods one morning this fall, I came across a perfectly formed spider's web bright with dew. The delicately woven strands reminded me that as we live and work for justice we spin out the thread of life that connects and supports us all.

The web of support that joins me to my friends is like a lifeline. Sometimes I can almost feel it — tiny golden threads tying my heart to the hearts of others. My passion for life, for justice, fueled by theirs.

These connections are often formed at gatherings of women of faith. It is there that I am able to laugh and cry, to speak the truth. To tell my story and let another share my journey.

Afterwards my life is never the same. I am a porous being. There are spaces in my soul like the open places in a web. Other people pass through me. I am changed and sometimes I am born again to a whole new way of being, of understanding myself, my work, and the world.

The dreams we spin need to be tied to something. The spider's web I saw was attached to the graceful curve at the end of a wild blackberry cane.

As we work together we can create and maintain a web of connection that will support us all.

— Jeanette Stokes,
"Women Empowered and Blessed"[2]

OUT OF HER OWN BODY,
SHE WEAVES THE WORLD

INTRODUCTION: Hopi Legend of Spiderwoman

> *Leader:* Spiderwoman is a Native American Goddess from a Hopi legend who is credited with the beginning of creation, since she wove woman and man. Spiderwoman was the first to create designs and to teach the Indian people how to weave. Every design she created had her spirit in it and every design contained a flaw so that her spirit could find its way out and be free.

SONG

"Rise Up, O Flame," from *Rise Up Singing*[3]

READINGS

To be read by two alternating or six individual voices.

Reading 1

In the beginning, as one of the old stories says, there was nothing but Spiderwoman. She spun two threads and where they crossed she sat singing and her singing made everything and held it all together.

I remember my mother, sitting at the center, holding us together. I remember the apartment in Chicago as eternally dark yellow. It seemed always to be dead winter. There was only one room with sufficient natural light. We called it the dining room because it was next to the kitchen, but we never ate at the big table in this room. This is the room, the room with the light where my mother sat with her three daughters.

She teaches us songs. We sing together, we lean together to her light. We listen to the radio, drawing pictures as we hear the serials. My mother sits at the table with us and sews. One afternoon the two of us are alone at the table. She is sewing, I am drawing. She is always silent when she sews. I am aware of the passing afternoon and of our being alone. It is a great happiness. I want the afternoon to last. I ask, "What do you think about when you sew?" "I don't think. I am remembering," she replies. "When I am sewing, I hold you all together." She then asks me what I think about when I draw. I tell her I do not think; I tell her I am drawing stories.

— Meinrad Craighead,
"Web," *The Mother's Song*[4]

Reading 2

WEAVING: Original activity of Websters:... constructing a context which sustains Sisters on the Otherworld Journey.... "All mother goddesses spin and weave.... Everything that is comes out of them: they weave the world tapestry out of genesis and demise, 'threads appearing and disappearing rhythmically.'"

—Helen Diner, *Mothers and Amazons:
The First Feminine History of Culture*[5]

Reading 3

WEBSTER: A woman whose occupation is to weave, esp. a Weaver of Words and Word-Webs. N.B.: The word "Webster" was Dis-covered by Judy Grahn, who has written:

> Webster is a word that formerly meant "female weaver," the "ster" ending indicating a female ancestor or female possession of the word. The word-weavers of recent centuries who have given us the oration of Daniel Webster and the dictionary listings of Merriam-Webster stem from English family names that once descended through the female line. Some great-great-grandmother gave them her last name, Webster, she-who-weaves.

—Judy Grahn, *The Queen of Wands*[6]

Reading 4

SPINNING: Gyn-Ecological creation; Dis-covering the lost thread of connectedness within the cosmos and repairing this thread in the process; whirling and twirling the threads of Life on the axis of Spinsters' own be-ing....

Reading 5

SPINSTER: A woman whose occupation is to Spin, to participate in the whirling movement of creation; one who has chosen her Self, who defines her Self by choice neither in relation to children nor to men; one who is Self-identified.

—Mary Daly, *Webster's First New
Intergalactic Wickedary of the English Language*[7]

Reading 6

[Charlotte:] "But cheer up, you don't need a web. Zuckerman supplies you with three big meals a day. Why should you worry about trapping food?" Wilbur signed. "You're ever so much cleverer and brighter than I am, Charlotte. I guess I was just trying to show off. Serves me right."

"You needn't feel too badly, Wilbur," she said. "Not many creatures can spin webs. Even men aren't as good at it as spiders, although they 'think' they're pretty good, and they'll 'try' anything. Did you ever hear of the Queensborough Bridge?" Wilbur shook his head. "Is it a web?"

"Sort of," replied Charlotte. "But do you know how long it took men to build it? Eight whole years. My goodness, I would have starved to death waiting that long. I can make a web in a single evening."

"What do people catch in the Queensborough Bridge — bugs?" asked Wilbur.

"No," said Charlotte. "They don't catch anything. They just keep trotting back and forth across the bridge thinking there is something better on the other side. If they'd hang head-down at the top of the thing and wait quietly, maybe something good would come along. But no — with men it's rush, rush, rush every minute. I'm glad I'm a sedentary spider."

— Excerpt from *Charlotte's Web*, by E. B. White[8]

UNISON READING

John 17:9–11, 20–23, 26

OUR RESPONSES

- on our role as Websters/Spinsters
- on interconnectedness, of the world and of women

Women are invited to speak one at a time. The first woman to speak holds a ball of red yarn in her hand. When she finishes speaking she waits for another woman to indicate a desire to speak and tosses the yarn to her. As this is repeated over and over, the group creates a giant web across the center of the circle, symbolizing their connection.

BLESSING OF OUR CONNECTIONS

O God, our Web-Weaver, we ask your blessing on the weaving of this web; on our creativity as we work together to design a web that will provide nourishment for our spirits, rest for our souls, and comfort for our bodies; a web that will be strong and flexible enough to encourage others to build webs of their own design. Amen.

— from "Women Empowered and Blessed"

...AND SHE RE-WEAVES...

MUSIC FOR REFLECTION

"Lydia's Song," words and music by Kathy and Robert Eddy[9]

WEAVING: A SYMBOL OF OUR PRAYERS

During the singing of this song, three women cut the web into pieces. Participants are invited to tie a piece of the yarn onto each other's wrists, to symbolize the blood of women who live in the midst of violence and the blood

*of Christ "which ties together in suffering and hope." This symbol has been
adopted by the Ecumenical Decade of Churches in Solidarity with Women,
sponsored by the World Council of Churches.*

...AND DRAWS EVERYTHING, AT THE END,
BACK INTO HERSELF

SONG

"Jubilate," Michael Praetorius, from *Rise Up Singing*[10]

FINAL BLESSING

Sovereign God, our Weaver, be with us as we weave,
bless each of us in the purpose for which we have created a web,
and bless the weaving when it is done. Amen.

—from "Women Empowered and Blessed"

•

SUGGESTED ALTERNATE HYMNS

"God of Many Names" (UMH)

NOTES

1. "A Circle Is Cast: Rounds, Chants, and Songs for Celebration and Ritual" by Libana. Available from Libana, Inc. P.O. Box 530, Cambridge, MA 02140.

2. Words for Reflection before Worship, Blessing of Our Connections, and Final Blessing are from "Women Empowered and Blessed," © 1990. The United Church of Christ Coordinating Center for Women in Church and Society, 700 Prospect Avenue, Cleveland, OH 44115.

3. *Rise Up Singing* (Sing Out Corporation, P.O. Box 5253, Bethlehem, PA 18015), 1988.

4. Excerpt from *The Mother's Song* by Meinrad Craighead © 1986. Published by Paulist Press, 997 MacArthur Blvd., Mahwah, NJ 07430. Used by permission of publisher.

5. Definition of "Weaving" from *Mothers and Amazons: The First Feminine History of Culture* by Helen Diner, © 1965, Julian Press.

6. Definition of "Webster" from *Queen of Wands* © 1982 by Judy Grahn. Published by The Crossing Press, Freedom, Calif. Used by permission.

7. Definitions of "Spinning" and "Spinster" from *Webster's First New Intergalactic Wickedary of the English Language* by Mary Daly, conjured in cahoots

PART II

Inclusive Worship for the Church Community

12

THE WORD MADE FLESH

(First Sunday after Christmas)

INTRODUCTION

After all the preparation for Advent and the excitement of Christmas, it is often difficult for a worship leader to find energy for the first Sunday after Christmas. But the Scripture texts for this week are so full of hope and excitement that we are caught up in the new visions of Jeremiah and John.

God is doing something new! God has been born again in each of us, and God is with us! We need not let the spiritual exaltation of Christmas slip away. The passages for this time are a gift to us, reminding us what God has done. Jeremiah, usually the prophet of doom and gloom, gives us words of hope and restoration: a theme that will be picked up in the New Testament by John. Our reason to celebrate, to feel as hopeful as we do, is confirmed. God has done a marvelous thing: we have a new gift of life! This is a message that no one tires of hearing. So much in our lives drains our spirits and works against hope. Now, unexpectedly, God has made all things new; and life and hope are restored! We do have reason to celebrate.

PREPARATION

This worship experience is designed to allow time for silent reflection as well as discussion and creativity. A table with materials for the "snowflake" project stands to one side of a circle of chairs. Materials include white construction paper, scissors, glue, tape, pencils, string, hole punchers, colored markers.

In the center of the circle is a table with communion elements set out as our visible reminder of hope renewed. A bare evergreen tree, on which the snowflakes will be hung, stands next to the communion table or behind it. Before worship four people are asked to be "Voices" for the Prayers of Confession.

•

GATHERING

> *Leader:* God speaks!
> with excitement!
> with enthusiasm!
> with new life!
>
> *People:* God is present!
> God is with us!
> nothing can separate us!
>
> *Leader:* Even when we feel unsure,
> unclear,
> confused,
> even when we feel broken to the core of our being —
>
> *People:* We hold fast to God's love,
> God's acceptance,
> we are always welcome in God's household.
>
> *Leader:* We will each, once again,
> feel like a well-watered garden.
> Full of life!
> Radiant in the sun!
>
> *People:* It will be good.
> It is good.

> — Rosemary C. Mitchell
> (adapted from Jer. 31:7–14)

SONG

"I Am the Light of the World," by Jim Strathdee, in *Songs of Shalom*

PRAYERS FOR ALL PEOPLE

> *Voice 1:* Who are we, God, that we should confess you?
> We can hardly speak for ourselves:
> How could we speak in your name?
> We believe in your word,
> but our minds are often full of doubt.
> We trust your promises,
> but our hearts are often fearful.
> We remember that we have been baptized,

but often forget to respond to your grace.
Captivate our minds, God,
and let your Spirit dwell in our hearts
that we may know the love
which you have given to us in your Son.

Response: God, we believe — forgive our unbelief.

Voice 2:   How can we call new disciples for you, God,
while our community, your church, is divided
and all too conformed to the pattern of this world?
We preach your power of love
while we succumb, like all others,
to the love of power.
We proclaim your justice
while we remain caught up in the structures
of injustice.
Awake in us the spirit of unity
that we may feel the pain of your body divided;
and yearn and reach out for fuller union with you
and with one another.
Inflame us with the power of your love
that it may consume the vanity of power.
Make us hunger and thirst for justice,
that our words may be given authority
as signs of your justice.

Response: God, we believe — forgive our unbelief.

Voice 3:   How can we sing your song, O God
in a strange land?
How can we witness to your all-embracing love
with lives full of painful contradictions?
How can we be ambassadors of reconciliation
in a world enslaved by sin and death,
where children suffer and starve,
and many labor in vain while a few live in luxury:
where, in the midst of our lives,
we dwell under the shadow of death?
What answer shall we give to the suffering
(what shall we say in our own hearts)
when they cry from the depths:
"Where now is your God?"

Response: God, we believe — forgive our unbelief.

Voice 4:   God, mysterious and hidden,
it is in our captivity that you reveal yourself

as the open door,
it is in the midst of our pain
that your suffering love heals us,
and it is in the depths of our despair
that you shine upon us
as the morning star of hope.
God crucified, God risen:
come transform the necessities
that are laid upon us
into freedom, joy, and praise everlasting.

Response: God, we believe — forgive our unbelief!
God, we believe — help our unbelief!

—*No Longer Strangers,*
World Council of Churches[1]

HEARING THE WORD OF GOD

John 1:1–18

INTERPRETING THE WORD OF GOD:
"Our Unique Gifts and Our Common Hopes"

The worship leader gives a very brief reflection on the Christmas Season as a time of hope discovered and reclaimed. The people present are invited to reflect on their hopes for this season.

What are you hoping for or what is your hope? Is it patience? Or understanding? Or attentiveness to others? Or enthusiasm for life? Or peace? Or faithfulness? What area of your life needs renewal or needs to be restored to new life?

The worship leader might read from or have some members prepare a favorite passage from one or more of the following books:

Frederick Buechner, *Wishful Thinking: A Theological ABC* (New York: Harper & Row, 1973).

———, *Whistling in the Dark: An ABC Theologized* (New York: Harper & Row, 1988).

J. Ruth Gendler, *The Book of Qualities* (New York: Harper & Row, 1984).

PERIOD OF SILENCE

SHARING THE WORD OF GOD

Invite people to share their insights, thoughts, and reflections in pairs or in small groups of four or five people. Participants are then invited to make a snowflake. On the snowflake they are asked to write their hope for this season.

Why a snowflake? Snowflakes are each unique and entirely distinctive from one another in size, shape, and design — just like each of us. Each one is distinctive and has beauty in its own right, but alone a snowflake melts immediately and is gone. That sometimes happens to our hopes. When individual snowflakes come together they begin to "stick" and stay with us. When our individual snowflakes of hope come together they transform a bare, empty tree into a tree of hope. Individually they are wonderful; together they form a new vision. That creation is like the coming together of our hopes. There is strength in numbers, and in sharing and combining our hopes and dreams.

After creating the snowflakes all are invited to hang their creations on the tree.

SONG

"O Jesus Christ, Life of the Earth," by Jane Parker Huber, in *A Singing Faith*

CELEBRATION OF COMMUNION:
A Meal of Hope and Renewal

Use a familiar communion liturgy.

SONG

"Love Divine, All Loves Excelling," *The Worshipbook*

CLOSING PRAYER (unison)

> O God, you have been present with us in this meal shared.
> Be with us always.
> We long to truly be your partners in creation.
> > Give us eyes to see.
> > Give us hearts to care.
> > Give us hands that reach out to lighten the burden.
> That others may know of your love and compassion.
> That hope may be renewed.
> For the sake of Christ. Amen.

— Rosemary C. Mitchell

BLESSING AND SCATTERING

●

SUGGESTED ALTERNATE HYMNS

"For Perfect Love So Freely Spent" (WB)

"God of the Ages, By Whose Hand" (WB)

"Hope of the World" (TPH, UMH, WB, HB, PH)

"O God Our Help in Ages Past" (UMH, WB, HB)

"What Child Is This" (TPH, UMH, WB, HB, PH)

NOTE

1. The Prayers for All People from *No Longer Strangers: A Resource for Women and Worship* by Iben Gjerding and Katherine Kinnamon, 1983, World Council of Churches Publications, P.O. Box 2100, 1211 Geneva 2, Switzerland. Used with permission.

13

CREATION IN THE WILDERNESS

(Lent)

INTRODUCTION

The inspiration for the content of this service of worship came from a sermon preached by the Rev. Yvonne Delk entitled "Freed to Follow."[1] James Weldon Johnson's sermon poem "Creation" is also recommended as a resource.[2]

In her sermon, Rev. Delk says the following:

> In the story of Jesus' own temptation, our Lord went into the wilderness obeying an experience that had little specific direction. The dove came, as did peace and an affirmation of who he was. But the voice that said who he was did not send down from heaven a list of detailed instructions. It said merely that he was affirmed as a beloved son. It did not outline goals and directions for the next thirty-six months. And the temptations that he fought as a human in the wilderness were specific. But when our Lord's temptation has ended, he goes back eighty-five miles to Capernaum and turning to two friends simply says "Follow me."
>
> The call to follow in the promised land is different from a call to follow in the wilderness. Following in the promised land is to bless and affirm what we see here as signs of God's reign. It is identifying so closely with the culture that we become culture's tool of conformity rather than Christ's instrument of transformation. Following in the promised land is to bless our nation right or wrong and to offer simplistic answers to complex questions.
>
> Following in the wilderness demands that we abandon our gods of arrogance, pride, nationality, class, culture, race, Protestant rule, in order to be carriers of God's grace and vision into the world. To follow in the wilderness is to abandon the nationally

99

defined God of imperial triumphalism and to affirm the covenanting God who freely chooses to enter a relationship with a people who are merely a band of slaves with no standing, no power, no influence in the world. This God is defined by freely offered compassion to those who by the world's definition are the helpless, the oppressed, and the dispossessed. This God exists in the margins where the suffering is most severe and offers us memory, hope, and compassion. This God calls us away from privatized religion that leaves behind any memory of the cost of discipleship and offers us an opportunity to be signs of hope and newness in the midst of the wilderness.

"Signs of hope and newness in the wilderness" can be a very jarring mixture of images. It is especially jarring as we pair the account of Jesus' temptation with the story of creation. But creation *can* emerge in the midst of a wilderness chaos: Jesus emerges from the wilderness experience strengthened, and prepared for his ministry. Instead of fearing the wilderness, we are allowed to embrace those times of wilderness wandering as the beginnings of creativity or a testing of ourselves in order to become the strong images of God intended by our Creator.

PREPARATION

In preparation for this service bulletins should be numbered "1," "2," or "3" for the Gathering Litany.

•

A STORY OF CREATION

  Leader: Once upon a time, in the beginning,
      a labor of love was undertaken.

  Group 1: It started with a sign,
      to show that something was about to happen.
      Light came forth from the deep darkness,
      bright, clear, and unmistakable.
      And it was very good.

  Group 2: At the second time, the waters were broken.
      At first, they gushed,
      then they dried to a trickle,
      and a space was created.
      It was exactly the right size.
      By now, the creation was well underway.
      And it was very good.

Group 3: At the third time, a cradle was made ready.
It was comfortable and beautiful and waiting.
And the food was prepared,
issuing sweetly and warmly
and in precisely the right measure
from the being of the laborer.
And it was very good.

Group 1: At the fourth time, rhythm was established.
Ebbing and flowing, contracting and expanding,
pain and joy, sun and moon, beginning and ending.
The labor of love progressed.
And it was very good.

Group 2: At the fifth time, there was ceaseless activity.
Fluttering like the wings of the dove.
Humming like the murmur of the dragonfly,
swimming like the darting golden fish,
wriggling like the lithe serpent,
leaping like the flashing deer,
surging like the mighty lion.
And it was very good.

Group 3: At the sixth time,
there was a momentary, endless hesitation.
Then a child was born.
And the child looked just like the one
who had given it life.
The child was born with the power
to create and to make decisions and to love.
The laborer looked at all
that had been accomplished and rejoiced.
For it was very good.

Unison: At the seventh time, the labor was finished.
The task was complete.
And the laborer rested,
for she was very, very tired.

— Kathy Galloway[3]

SONG

"Creating God, Your Fingers Trace," by Jeffrey Rowthorn,
in *Everflowing Streams*

UNISON PRAYER

> God our lover, you draw us to search for you;
> you give us clues to your presence in creation;
> we find you in each other's faces,
> in the challenge and intimacy of human love.
> Yet always you elude our grasp;
> familiar and yet always strange,
> you both comfort and disturb our lives.
> We surrender all our images of you,
> and offer ourselves to your darkness;
> that you may enable us to become your likeness
> more than what we can imagine or conceive.

— Janet Morley, *Celebrate Women*[4]

CREATED IN GOD'S IMAGE IN THE WILDERNESS

Genesis 2:4–3:7

INTERPRETING THE WORD OF GOD

Rolled out on the floor are long sheets of newsprint. Each person is invited to lie on a section of the paper and have his/her outline drawn (from the waist up); each then writes his/her own name across the shoulders of the image. Others are invited to write on this "image of God" the qualities this person brings to God's creation.

ONE OF GOD'S OWN IN THE WILDERNESS

Matthew 4:1–11

SONG

"Christ Jesus Knew a Wilderness," by Jane Parker Huber,
in *Joy in Singing*

INTERPRETING THE WORD OF GOD

In small groups have a discussion around these questions:

- How do you describe "the wilderness"?

- What kinds of experience have tempted or tested you?

- What experiences can you describe from your own life that you know have made you stronger, healthier, energized?

PRAYERS OF THE PEOPLE

SONG

"Lead on, O Cloud of Yahweh," words by Ruth Duck,
Everflowing Streams

BLESSING AND BENEDICTION

•

SUGGESTED ALTERNATE HYMNS

"Awake My Soul, Stretch Every Nerve" (vs. 1, 2, 4,) (TPH, UMH, WB, HB, PH)

"Come Holy Ghost, Our Souls Inspire" (vs. 1, 2, 3,) (HB, PH, TPH, UMH, WB)

"Guide Me, O Thou Great Jehovah" (TPH, UMH, WB, HB, PH)

"Jesus Calls Us O'er the Tumult" (TPH, UMH, WB, HB, PH)

"Many Gifts, One Spirit" (UMH)

"O Love That Wilt Not Let Me Go" (TPH, UMH, WB, HB, PH)

"O Praise the Gracious Power" (TPH)

"Spirit Divine, Attend Our Prayers" (TPH, WB, HB, PH)

NOTES

1. Excerpt from sermon, "Freed to Follow" by Yvonne Delk, from *The Princeton Seminary Bulletin* 9, no. 1 (1990). Used by permission of author.

2. "Creation" by James Weldon Johnson from *God's Trombones* (New York: Viking Press, 1927).

3. "A Story of Creation" by Kathy Galloway, Iona Community, Scotland. Used with permission of author.

4. The Unison Prayer by Janet Morley from *Celebrate Women*, edited by Janet Morley and Hannah Ward, WIT/MOW, 1986. Used by permission.

14

LENTEN LIFE

(Lent)

INTRODUCTION

Ezekiel brings to mind the idea of being scattered, broken, cut off—
life moments that leave us feeling "dead." So much in our daily lives
is death-dealing: events and encounters "break us" and we feel cut out
from any source of community or from God's life-giving presence.

The children's game "Musical Chairs" can be a metaphor of that
feeling of being "cut out"; its use makes this an exciting service in
which all ages can participate. (Children and youth especially seem
to connect with that feeling of being "cut out" of the game, since
they often experience this when "sides" are chosen and someone is
the last to be picked.) With communion as a part of this liturgy the
metaphor of the game is transformed, with appropriate music, to one
of community building.

All ages can participate not only in the game, but also in animated
discussion of the feelings involved. The depth of conversation that
follows is impressive. Older persons in the group remember playing
the childhood game of "Musical Chairs" as "Marching to Jerusalem,"
making an interesting connection with Lent.

PREPARATION

Musical Chairs: When the game begins, participants are seated in chairs
set in a line. Each chair is occupied. As recorded music is played all
rise and walk around the line of chairs. The leader removes one chair
as they walk. When the music is suddenly turned off, each participant
sits in the nearest vacant chair. One player is left standing. That player
then leaves the game, taking one chair, and the cycle is repeated.

As the game is played out, chairs are scattered around the room.
When the game ends, people are seated in these scattered chairs. The
winner is applauded and discussion begins.

Readers for the Scripture lesson should be recruited in advance.

•

GATHERING WORDS (unison)

O God, we do not always know why we are here.
We are often unsure of our purpose on earth.
Sometimes we hope to catch a glimpse of who you are
through the eyes of your startling vision,
which images *us* as your caring, compassionate people.

—Rosemary C. Mitchell

SONG

"Give Thanks to God, the Source of Life," by Robert Bachelder,
in *Everflowing Streams*

FIRST SCRIPTURE READING

Ezekiel 37:1–10

THE METAPHOR OF MUSICAL CHAIRS
(Part I)

The people are seated in the formation of the game "Musical Chairs." An introduction should refresh memories on the rules of the game (see above).
    When the game ends and the winner is applauded, some observations can be made:

- They are now people scattered and dispersed. Alone, they will become lifeless. There is only one winner, and what has been won?
- How might this game be interpreted as a metaphor for Ezekiel's vision of the valley of dry bones?

Move to the time of confession after participants have had an opportunity to reflect, but while everyone still remains scattered around the room.

CONFESSING THOSE TIMES WE FALL SHORT
OF WHAT GOD INTENDS FOR US

    Leader: As we consider the dry bones of Ezekiel's vision...
    as we consider the dead body of Lazarus...
    we realize that sometimes we are dry, lifeless,
    despairing of our faith and despairing of our actions.
    Hear our prayers, O God.

    All: O God, in your presence we recognize
    that we ourselves are not fully alive.
    We often give up.

We often give in to the sin of despair;
we have been lifeless, not life-giving.
Like dry bones we lack ability.
We are brittle.
If asked to bend, we break.
Like the neighbors and friends of Lazarus,
we have no hope of new life.
May your spirit of power fill us.
May our faith become active.
May we be the people who breathe new life
into dead surroundings,
that the name of God may be glorified.
Amen.

— Rosemary C. Mitchell

SECOND READING

Adapted from John 11:1–45

Voice 1: Now a certain man was ill, Lazarus of Bethany, in the village of Mary and her sister Martha.

Women: It was Mary who anointed the Lord with ointment and wiped his feet with her hair, whose brother Lazarus was ill.

Voice 1: So the sisters sent to him, saying:

Women: "Lord, he whom you love is ill."

Voice 1: But when Jesus heard it he said,

Voice 2: "This illness is not unto death; it is for the glory of God so that the Son of God may be glorified by means of it."

Voice 1: Now Jesus loved Martha and her sister and Lazarus. So when he heard that he was ill, he stayed two days longer in the place where he was. Then after this he said to the disciples:

Voice 2: "Let us go into Judea again."

Voice 1: The disciples said to him:

All: "Rabbi, the Jews were but now seeking to stone you, and are you going there again?"

Voice 2: "Are there not twelve hours in the day? If any one walks in the day, he does not stumble, because he sees the light of this world. But if any one walks in the night, he stumbles, because the light is not in him. Our friend Lazarus has fallen asleep, but I go to awake him out of sleep."

All: "Lord, if he has fallen asleep, he will recover."

Voice 1: Now Jesus had spoken of his death, but they thought that he meant taking rest in sleep. Then Jesus spoke plainly:

Voice 2: "Lazarus is dead, and for your sake I am glad that I was not there, so that you may believe. But let us go to him."

Voice 1: Thomas the twin, said to his fellow disciples:

Voice 3: "Let us also go, that we may die with him."

Voice 1: Now when Jesus came, he found that Lazarus had already been in the tomb four days. Bethany was near Jerusalem, about two miles away, and many of the Jews had come to Martha and Mary to console them concerning their brother. When Martha heard that Jesus was coming, she went and met him, while Mary sat in the house. Martha said to Jesus:

Women: "Lord, if you had been here, my brother would not have died. And even now I know that whatever you ask from God, God will give you."

Voice 2: "Your brother will rise again."

Women: "I know that he will rise again in the resurrection at the last day."

Voice 2: "I am the resurrection and the life. Whoever believes in me, though they die, yet shall they live, and whoever lives and believes in me shall never die. Do you believe this?"

Women: "Yes, Lord, I believe that you are the Christ, the Son of God, He who is coming into the world."

Voice 1: When she had said this, she went and called her sister Mary, saying quietly:

Women: "The Teacher is here and is calling for you."

Voice 1: And when Mary heard it she rose quickly and went to him. Now Jesus had not yet come to the village, but was still in the place when Martha had met him. When the Jews who were with her in the house, consoling her saw Mary rise quickly and go out, they followed her, supposing that she was going to the tomb to weep there. Then Mary, when she came where Jesus was and saw him, fell at his feet, saying to him:

Women: "Lord, if you had been here my brother would not have died."

Voice 1: When Jesus saw her weeping, and the Jews who came with her also weeping he was deeply moved in spirit and troubled, and said:

Voice 2: "Where have you laid him?"

Women: "Lord, come and see."

Voice 2: Some of the Jews said, "See how he loved him!" and others said, "Could not he who opened the eyes of the blind man have kept this man from dying?"

Voice 1: Jesus was deeply moved again, and came to the tomb; it was a cave, and a stone lay upon it.

Voice 2: "Take away the stone."

All: "Lord, by this time there will be an odor, for he has been dead four days."

Voice 2: "Did I not tell you that if you would believe you would see the glory of God?

"God, I thank thee that thou hast heard me. I knew that thou hearest me always, but I have said this on account of the people standing by, that they may believe that thou didst send me.

"Lazarus, come out!"

Voice 1: The dead man came out, his hands and feet bound with bandages, and his face wrapped with a cloth.

Voice 2: "Unbind him! And let him go!"

Voice 1: Many of the Jews therefore, who had come with Mary and had seen what he did, believed in him; but some of them went to the Pharisees and told them what Jesus had done. So the chief priests and the Pharisees gathered the council and said:

All: "What are we to do? For this man performs many signs, if we let him go on thus, every one will believe in him, and the Romans will come and destroy both our holy place and our nation."

Voice 1:   But one of them, Caiaphas, who was the high priest that year, said to them:

Voice 3:   "You know nothing at all; you do not understand that it is expedient for you that one man should die for the people, and that the whole nation should not perish."

Voice 1:   He did not say this of his own accord, but being high priest that year he prophesied that Jesus should die for the nation, and not for the nation only, but to gather into one the children of God who are scattered abroad. So from that day they took counsel on how to put him to death.

THE METAPHOR OF MUSICAL CHAIRS
(Part II)

THE LIFE/GAME REVERSED

Since the end of the "game" of Musical Chairs, the winner has been seated in the winner's seat. At this point the game is played in reverse, beginning with the winner. In the center of the room is the communion table with the elements set out. The winner is invited to approach another person in the room, greet them with the words:

> "The game is over,
> Life begins.
> The peace of Christ be with you."

and to bring that person (with his or her chair) back to the center. Then they both go to two other persons and repeat the sequence. At the end the entire group is seated in a circle around the communion table. When the circle is completed, the musician plays "The Miracle of Life" or another appropriate song or hymn that speaks of life in community.

TIME OF REFLECTION

• How is new life together different?

SONG

"We Gather Round the Table Now," by Jane Parker Huber, in *A Singing Faith*

CELEBRATION OF THE LORD'S SUPPER

INVITATION

Leader: Friends, this is the joyful feast of the people of God!

People: As members of God's household we gather, from east and west, from north and south. We gather from houses and apartments, from cities, suburbs, and farms. We gather with the whole host of witnesses to sit at Christ's table, a glimpse of God's heavenly banquet.

Leader: This is Christ's table. Christ bids all to share this feast, that all might be renewed and strengthened.

        Christ invites us with our broken dreams, our hurts and bruises, our disappointments, our loss of self-esteem, to come to this table to find love, hope, and trust.

People: We bring our very selves into Christ's presence.

        We stand before God confused or tired or beaten down.

        We pray for the gift of Christ's healing grace that our souls might be inspired to live again.

Leader: According to the Gospel, the Risen Christ was at table with his friends, people confused and scared of what the future would hold. Christ took the bread and blessed it and gave it to them. And their eyes were open, they recognized him, and their lives were forever changed.

Leader: Lift up your hearts!

People: We lift them up to God!

Leader: Give thanks to God!

People: For God's love is everlasting!

PRAYER OF THANKSGIVING

Leader: O God, we acknowledge before you our common debt of gratitude; we are people of particular traditions and cultures, we are inheritors of grace and strength forged not with our own devices but bestowed by those who have gone before us.

People: Eternal God, may we who owe our spiritual blessings to ancestors both familial and spiritual, walk in your way as those who are indebted to your grace.

Leader: Lift us, O God, to keen insight into our task for this day. As Christ was raised in power, may we be empowered to do your work of reconciliation.

As Christ offered hope to those in despair, may we be life-giving to those who are hopeless.

As Christ loved without counting the cost may we continue to reach out to a hurting world. Therefore, with all the saints who in every age have shown Christ's love in acts of justice, peace, and healing, we praise you saying:

People: Holy, holy, holy God,
God of power and might.
Heaven and earth are full of your glory.
Hosanna in the highest.
Blessed is the one who comes in the name of God.
Hosanna in the highest.

Leader: Blessed is Christ, who is known to us in the breaking of the bread; who on the night he was betrayed, took bread, gave thanks, broke it, and said: "This is my body, which is for you. Do this to remember me."

In the same way Jesus took the cup after supper and when he had given thanks he said: "This is my blood of the new covenant, shed for you and for many. Whenever you drink it, do this for the remembrance of me."

Friends, these are the gifts of God for the people of God!

Unison: *The Lord's Prayer*

THE GIFTS OF GOD FOR THE PEOPLE OF GOD

The elements are distributed around the circle.

CLOSING PRAYER AND PEACE

Leader: We give thanks for this meal shared in the spirit of Christ, who makes us new and strong, who brings us life eternal.

People: We praise you, God, for granting us the peace that passes all understanding.

Leader: May the peace of Christ be with each of you.

People: And also with you.

SONG

"I Am the Resurrection," by Ray Repp, in *Songs*[1]

BLESSING AND SCATTERING

•

SUGGESTED ALTERNATE HYMNS

"Amazing Grace" (WB)

"Become to Us the Living Bread" (WB)

"Christ Is Made the Sure Foundation" (WB)

"Come Down, O Love Divine" (WB)

"Come, O Come, Great Quickening Spirit" (WB)

"Jesus Calls Us" (WB)

"Love Divine, All Loves Excelling" (WB)

"Take Thou Our Minds, Dear Lord" (WB)

NOTE

1. "I Am the Resurrection," by Ray Repp, in *Songs*, compiled by Yohann Anderson, published by Songs and Creations, Inc., P.O. Box 7, San Anselmo, CA 94960.

15

THE SERVANT KING

(Passion Sunday)

INTRODUCTION

How do we understand leadership? Was Jesus a leader? How do we understand power? How was Jesus powerful? Power and leadership issues seem to be a common topic of discussion, both in religious circles and in the secular world. Robert K. Greenleaf has written a series of essays on "Servant Leadership." One of his essays, "The Servant as Religious Leader," offers interesting insights for Passion Sunday, as we contemplate Jesus as servant and as king. We must struggle with the implications of both as Holy Week unfolds.

Greenleaf writes:

> One test of any kind of leadership is: Do leaders enjoy a mutual relationship with followers? Are these followers numerous enough and constant enough to make an effective force of their effort? The leader, if in fact a leader, is always attached to an effective force of people. Among those who are normally followers are those who, from time to time, sometimes in major ways, will also lead. The titular leader gives continuity and coherence to an endeavor in which many may lead.... An additional test for servant leaders is: Are they seekers? and... Do those served grow as persons: do they, while being served, become healthier, wiser, freer, more autonomous, more likely themselves to become servants? And, what is the effect on the least privileged person in society; will she or he benefit, or at least, not be further deprived?[1]

The focus of this service is our search for an understanding of leadership and power. How do we describe Jesus? What then is our relationship to Jesus? And what then is our relationship with those with whom we live and work?

What can we learn from a life led as both servant and king? The worship leader must also struggle with the meaning of leadership and power in ministry. We are in ministry "with" those whom we are called

113

to serve: that is, we must be both leaders and servants. What are the implications for life together in a congregation?

PREPARATION

Preparation for this service includes printing in the worship bulletin the Scripture readings and the words to "Ride On, Ride On, in Majesty." Bulletins are marked with numbers from 1 to 6 to designate each person's assignment.

The room is arranged with chairs in six circles. There is therefore no need to rearrange chairs for the discussion.

•

GATHERING WORDS

Leader: Jesus set his face resolutely toward Jerusalem.

People: We gather this day to be strengthened. Should there come a day when we must stand fast against the forces of evil, or say "No" to a terrible injustice, help us not be broken by the consequences of our decision or action, even though a dream we followed lies in fragments at our feet.

Leader: Let us worship God and celebrate the arrival of the "Servant-King."

SONG

"Here He Comes," by Richard Avery and Donald Marsh, in *Avery and Marsh Songbook*[2]

CONFESSION AND ACCEPTANCE

Confession by Worship Leader

O God, I give thanks for the privilege of gathering this day with your disciples.

Help me to see myself as they see me, to know myself as you know me.

Forgive me for my impulsive moments, inspired to declare great things — yet ready instantly to forsake you.

Forgive my resentful times, disappointed at the high cost of discipleship and quiet ministry of love.

Forgive my tired days when I am eager to watch and pray, but not strong enough to stay awake and share your suffering.

Forgive me when I am only mildly effective because I have not prayed enough.

When I am distracted trying to carry out old ways in new places, forgive
  my times of jealousy and discontent.
For Christ's sake. Amen.

Forgiveness by Congregation

You are valued as you are, for we have the assurance that Reality revealed in the "Person-for-others" accepts and loves even the
  unworthy.
Receive this gift, live freely, "sin boldly" secure in this grace.

Confession by Congregation

O God, we confess our slowness to see the good in our brothers and
  sisters and to see the evil in ourselves.
We confess our blindness to the sufferings of others and our slowness
  to be taught by our own suffering.
We confess our failure to apply to ourselves the standards of conduct
  we demand of others.
We confess our complacency toward wrongs that do not touch us and
  our oversensitivity to those that do.
We confess our hardness of heart toward our brothers' and sisters'
  faults and our readiness to make allowances for our own.
We confess our unwillingness to believe that you have called us to a
  small work, and others to a great one.

Forgiveness by Worship Leader

O God, who knows every human fault,
yet sees every potential glory,
who once did share a life with those whose faltering ways we know in
  our own hearts,
be ever with us — ever blessing and ever blest among us.

— *The Sycamore Book*[3]

THE PEACE

Leader: This is God's house, a place of peace.
a place where we befriend one another
in the name of Christ.

People: We enter strangers. We leave as friends.

Leader: Let us greet one another
as a sign of God's peace
and Christ's friendship.
May the peace of Christ be with each of you.

People: And also with you.

— Rosemary C. Mitchell

WE HEAR THE WORD OF GOD

Group 1:   Luke 9:51–56

All sing: "Ride On! Ride On! in Majesty" (verse 1),
The Worshipbook

Group 2:   Psalm 31:9–16

All sing: "Ride On! Ride On! in Majesty" (verse 2)

Group 3:   Isaiah 50:4–9a

All sing: "Ride On! Ride On! in Majesty" (verse 3)

Group 4:   Luke 18:31–34

All sing: "Ride On! Ride On! in Majesty" (verse 4)

Group 5:   Philippians 2:5–11

All sing: "Ride On! Ride On! in Majesty" (verse 1)

Group 6:   Luke 19:28–40

WE INTERPRET THE WORD OF GOD

In their groups people are asked to focus on their particular Scripture reading and to discuss their understandings of leadership and power. Questions to consider are:

- How is Jesus a powerful leader for you during the events of today and this week?

- In your mind, what are the characteristics of power and leadership?

After fifteen minutes in small groups people are invited to share their insights about the texts and their understandings of servant leadership, with the entire group.

SONG

"Jesus Calls Us," *The Worshipbook*

BLESSING AND SCATTERING

•

SUGGESTED ALTERNATE HYMNS

"Art Thou Weary" (HB)

"Awit Sa Dapit Hapon" (When Twilight Comes) (TPH)

"Beneath the Cross of Jesus" (HB, PH, TPH, UMH, WB)

"Here I Am, Lord" (TPH, UMH)

"Hope of the World" (UMH, WB, HB, PH)

"You Servants of God" (UMH, WB, HB, PH)

"In the Hour of Trial" (HB, PH)

"Jesu, Jesu, Fill Us with Your Love" (TPH, UMH)

NOTES

1. Excerpt reprinted with permission from "The Servant as Religious Leader" by Robert K. Greenleaf. Copyright by the Robert K. Greenleaf Center, 1100 W. 42nd St., Ste. 321, Indianapolis, IN 46208.

2. "Here He Comes," by Avery and Marsh from *The Avery and Marsh Songbook*, published by Proclamation Productions, Inc. Orange Square, Port Jervis, NY 12771.

3. The Confession and Acceptance are from *The Sycamore Book*, published by the Sycamore Community and the STS Press, 718 Glenn Rd., State College, PA 16803. Used with permission.

16

THE WITNESS TO LIFE
(Easter)

INTRODUCTION

Of all the observances of the Christian faith, Easter may be the day of our most joyous certainty *and* our deepest doubt — and the day we feel them in one and the same heartbeat, if we are truly honest with ourselves. This, after all, is what faith is about, since total certainty would not be "faith," which is "the assurance of things hoped for, the conviction of things not seen" (Heb. 11:1).

The brilliance of the Easter story is that it contains such a multi-faceted proclamation of Life's triumph over death. The stone, the empty shroud, the angels' appearance and announcement, Jesus' own prior promise, the experience of "faithful doubters" — none of these, taken alone, is adequate "proof" of veracity of this astonishing good news. Taken together, and with the intimations of the Spirit in our lives, they provide a powerful signpost — pointing us toward, and inviting us into, the leap of *faith* required in order to believe.

PREPARATION

Since Easter is not ultimately about "pie in the sky when you die" but about the power of Life that begins here and now in the heart of the *world*, the choice of worship setting is crucial to its full meaning. Here more than ever, medium and message are of one piece. How will *this* particular worshipping community place the Easter proclamation in the heart of its world? For rural congregations, the "heart of the world" may well be the spaciousness of a pasture or a dormant field, while urban churches may find a city park (or parking lot!) the perfect setting, and suburban worshippers may gather in the center of a mall.

Wherever the setting, *spaciousness* is an important element for Easter worship, both for the metaphor of the "breathing room" the Gospel offers and for the capacity to allow worshippers to move physically — that is, to "take a stand." While much traditional worshipping is done in the confined space of a pew, an essential part of this celebration is the opportunity for each person to confess her/his faith *bodily* by coming forward to the Table at her/his chosen moment, thereby "giv[ing] answer for the hope that is in you."

The original setting for this Easter service was St. Joseph's Park in Rochester, New York — the flagstone courtyard (formerly a narthex) and towering granite walls and bell-tower of a center-city Roman Catholic cathedral that was destroyed by fire in 1974. After the opening litany, worshippers entered the enclosed courtyard (which is open to the sky and, on one side, to a business-district skyline) through large iron gates where once there were great church doors. The setting superimposed rich images of ruin and new life, empty tomb, marketplace, and holy space — a perfect combination to express the inexpressible nature of this day!

At the center of the worship space stands a round folding table, to serve as a communion table, covered with a white cloth and set with communion elements.

•

CALL TO WORSHIP: Isaiah 65:17–25

Voice 1: For behold, I create new heavens and a new earth; and the former things shall not be remembered or come into mind. But be glad and rejoice for ever in that which I create; for behold, I create Jerusalem a rejoicing, and its people a joy.

RESPONSE: "He Has Arisen, Alleluia"[1]

Cantor: He has arisen, Alleluia,
rejoice and praise him, Alleluia;
for our Redeemer burst from the tomb,
even from death dispelling its gloom.

Congregation: Let us sing praise to him with endless joy,
death's fearful sting he has come to destroy
our sins forgiving, alleluia,
Jesus is living: alleluia.

Voice 2: I will rejoice in Jerusalem, and be glad in my people; no more shall be heard in it the sound of weeping and the cry of distress. No more shall there be in it an infant that lives but a few days, or an old person who does not fill out a lifetime, for the child shall die a hundred years old....

Cantor: For three long days the grave did its worst,
until its strength by God was dispersed.
He who gives life did death undergo,
and in its conquest his might did show.

Congregation: "Let us sing praise to him . . ." etc.

Voice 3: They shall build houses and inhabit them; they shall plant vineyards and eat their fruit. They shall not build and another inhabit; they shall not plant and another eat; for like the days of a tree shall the days of my people be, and my chosen shall long enjoy the work of their hands.

Cantor: The angel said to them, "Do not fear,
you look for Jesus who is not here.
See for yourselves the tomb is all bare;
only the grave cloths are lying there."

Congregation: "Let us sing praise to him . . ." etc.

Voice 4: They shall not labor in vain, or bear children for calamity; for they shall be the offspring of the blessed of God, and their children with them. Before they call I will answer, while they are yet speaking I will hear.

Cantor: Go spread the news, he's not in the grave,
He has arisen us all to save.
Jesus' redeeming labors are done.
Even the battle with sin is won."

Congregation: "Let us sing praise to him . . ." etc.

Voice 5: The wolf and the lamb shall feed together, the lion shall eat straw like the ox; and dust shall be the serpent's food. They shall not hurt or destroy in all my holy mountain, says the Lord.

Cantor: He has arisen to set us free.
Alleluia, to him praises be.
The power of Satan no longer binds,
nor can enslave the thoughts of our minds.

Congregation: "Let us sing praise to him . . ." etc.

PRAYER OF ADORATION

Here the congregation is invited to move inside the gates to the inner courtyard or park area and gather in a large circle for the prayer.

THE CHALLENGE: 1 Corinthians 15:12–20

Leader: Our setting this morning is not unlike the *agora*, the marketplace, where Paul was tried. All of *us*, in a sense, are "on trial" to display the faith of the resurrection in the modern day.

After explaining this setting, the leader asks the group to participate in an experience of "passing on the Word" much akin to our childhood game of "Secrets," or "Whispering Down the Lane." The leader whispers a message into the ears of each person flanking her to the right and left; each in turn whispers it on to a neighbor, and so on around the circle. The "test" at the end is to report aloud what message arrived from either direction. The words, which are from 1 Peter 3:14 — "Always be ready to give answer for the hope that is in you" — usually "arrive" in unrecognizable form, lending the opportunity to reflect as a community on the importance of our responsibility in carrying the message of new life!

THE "PROOF": Luke 24:1–12

Here, listening to the account of Easter according to Luke, there is opportunity indeed to "give answer for the hope that is in you." Participants are asked to consider which "witness" they take as the foundation of their Easter conviction and, when that witness is read aloud, to move from the periphery of the space, where they have been standing, into the center to gather around the communion table. Two voices (perhaps a man and a woman), might be invited to announce each "witness" and to read the text describing it — allowing appropriate pauses for worshippers to move to the table.

The Witness of the Stone: Luke 24:1–2

Very early on Sunday morning, the women [who had come with Jesus from Galilee] took the burial spices they had prepared and went to the tomb. They found that the stone had been rolled away from the entrance to the tomb;

The Witness of the Empty Shroud: Luke 24:3

but when they entered, they did not find the body of the Lord Jesus.

The Witness of the Angels: Luke 24:4–5a

As they stood there, perplexed, suddenly beside them appeared two men in clothes that gleamed. The women were frightened and bowed their faces to the ground.

The Witness of Their Words: Luke 24:5b

But the men said to them, "Why do you search among the dead for one who lives?"

The Witness of Jesus' Words: Luke 24:6–8

"Remember what Jesus told you while he was still in Galilee: that the Chosen One must be given over to the hands of sinners, and be crucified, and must rise again on the third day."

Then the women remembered Jesus' words.

The Witness of Those Who Believe for None of These Reasons: Luke 24:9–11

And returning from the tomb, they told all this to the Eleven and to all the others. Those who told this were Mary Magdalene, Joanna, and Mary (the mother of James), and the rest of the women with them. But the apostles considered their words nonsense, and did not believe the women.

The Witness of the "Faithful Doubters": Christian Agnostics

There are also those who, joining with Thomas, declare "I believe: help my unbelief" — or those for whom *no* witness is relevant — who choose to follow Christ's company *anyway*; and here *they* are invited to come forward.

SONG

The Angels Rolled the Stone Away

O the angels rolled the stone away,
O the angels rolled the stone away,
'Twas on that Easter Sunday morning
That the angels rolled the stone away.[2]

THE PEACE

CELEBRATING THE EUCHARIST

The Invitation

Friends, welcome to the joyful feast of the people of God!

May our gathering at the Lord's table be like the experience of two disciples that first Easter day:

On their way to a village named Emmaus, as they discussed all that had happened around their teacher's death, Jesus drew near and walked with them. But their eyes were kept from recognizing him, even when he spoke.

When they came to the village they urged the stranger to stay and have supper with them. And while they were at table together, Jesus took the bread and blessed and broke it, and gave it to them. And their eyes were opened, and they recognized him!

Song

"Jesus Christ Is Risen Today," *The Worshipbook*

Prayers of Thanksgiving

Words of Institution

Sharing the Bread and the Cup

PRAYER OF PRAISE

> Lord of such amazing surprises
> as put a catch in my breath
> and wings on my heart,
> I praise you for this joy,
> too great for words,
> but not for tears and songs and sharing:
> for this mercy
> that blots out my betrayals
> and bids me begin again...
>
> for this YES
> to life and laughter,
> to love and lovers,
> and to my unwinding self;
> for this kingdom
> unleashed in me and I in it forever,
> and no dead ends to growing,
> to choices,
> to chances,
> to calls to be just;
> no dead ends to living,
> to making peace,
> to dreaming dreams,
> to being glad of heart;
> for this resurrection madness
> which is wiser than I
> and in which I see
> how great you are,
> how full of grace.
> Alleluia!

— Ted Loder, excerpted from
Guerrillas of Grace[3]

SONG

"Let Us Talents and Tongues Employ"; words: Fred Kaan;
tune adapted by Doreen Potter, *The Presbyterian Hymnal*

BENEDICTION

•

SUGGESTED ALTERNATE HYMNS

"Christ Is Alive!" (TPH, UMH)

"Christ Is Risen! Shout Hosanna!" (TPH, UMH)

NOTES

1. "He Has Arisen, Alleluia" (Mfurahini, Haleluya) is a Haya melody from Tanzania with words by Kiongozia and Bernard Kyamanywa. The music is found in *Prayers and Poems, Songs and Stories: Worship and Meditation Resources for Easter and for the Ecumenical Decade Churches in Solidarity with Women 1988-1998*. Used by permission of the Lutheran World Federation.

2. "The Angels Rolled the Stone Away," Spiritual, arr. by Donald P. Hustad in *Faith, Folk, and Festivity*. Arr. © 1969 by Hope Publishing Co., Carol Stream, IL 60188. All rights reserved. Used by permission.

3. The Prayer of Praise is reprinted from *Guerrillas of Grace: Prayers for the Battle* by Ted Loder © 1984 LuraMedia, Inc., San Diego, Calif. Used by permission.

17

THE BAPTISM OF MADELYN CLAIRE BROWN

(Pentecost/Bringing a Child into the Faith Community)

INTRODUCTION

Scripture offers us three primary images for how we become and are becoming children of God: by our very createdness (Genesis and the prophets), by "receiving the spirit of adoption" (Romans), and by rebirth "from above" (John's Gospel). The creation of a baptismal service for little Madelyn Claire Brown — a process very much influenced and shaped by her parents — emphasized the interconnectedness of each of these images.

It was important to all of us that this celebration of the sacrament be rooted in a passionate belief in the goodness of our being, not in "original sin" but in "original blessing," to follow the thought of creation theologians like Matthew Fox. It was essential that the sacrament be an act of the whole gathered community: incorporating not only the scriptural image of adoption into the family of faith but also the Reformed understanding of infant baptism as an act by which the church makes a corporate commitment to nurture the child in faith. At the same time, we wished to reaffirm that the work of the Spirit in the lives of our children cannot be controlled or directed by *us*, but is wonderful mystery and "amazing grace."

PREPARATION

Since the symbolic focus of this service is the "baptismal font," the worship space should be arranged with the font or bowl containing the waters of baptism in the center. We covered the table with an antique lace cloth and invited the child's parents to provide a bowl that might have particular significance within their family—one that, years later, might be passed on to Madelyn for special use in her own household.

Madelyn's parents, Carol and Jeff, chose the Wendell Berry poem "Our Children, Coming of Age"—which they personally had found meaningful—to be read during worship by a mentor/friend in the congregation; the text of that poem was printed on the bulletin cover. Worshippers were seated in a large circle of chairs with the "font" as focal point. We often invite the younger children of the community to gather close to the "action" during infant baptism, so that they are able to see and take part in the sacrament. This means inviting them into the center of the circle, or up front, if the worship space is a traditional one with rows of pews.

•

WELCOME

INVOCATION OF GOD'S SPIRIT

All sing: Come, Spirit, come and be a new reality.
Your touch is guarantee of love alive in me.

Side 1:   Come, Spirit: as light in darkness...

Side 2:   Come, Spirit: as rain in drought...

Side 1:   Come, Spirit: as warmth in winter...

Side 2:   Come, Spirit: and bail us out.

All sing: Come, Spirit, come and be a new reality.
Your touch is guarantee of love alive in me.

Side 1:   Come: visit the unenlightened...

Side 2:   Come: slake our staggering thirst...

Side 1:   Come: establish the ways of justice...

Side 2:   Come: be with us through the worst.

All sing: Come, Spirit, come and be a new reality.
Your touch is guarantee of love alive in me.

Side 1:   Come, Spirit: as healing and wholeness...

Side 2:   Come, Spirit: as life-giving food...

Side 1:   Come, Spirit: as hope in oppression...

Side 2:   Come, Spirit: as all that is good.

All sing: Come, Spirit, come and be a new reality.
Your touch is guarantee of love alive in me.

Side 1: Come: banish discrimination...

Side 2: Come: wash its wounds away...

Side 1: Come: break the bread of freedom...

Side 2: Come: declare a holy day.

All sing: Come, Spirit, come and be a new reality.
Your touch is guarantee of love alive in me.

Side 1: Come, Spirit: you are the victory...

Side 2: Come, Spirit: you are the grace...

All say: Come, Spirit: you are the reason
this gathering is a holy place.
Come, Spirit, come!

All sing: Come, Spirit, come and be a new reality.
Your touch is guarantee of love alive in me.

— Miriam Therese Winter,
WomanPrayer, WomanSong[1]

PRAYER OF THANKS

O God, we rejoice in your grace, given and received.
We thank you that you claim us
and are working in our lives
to strengthen, encourage, and guide us.
We praise you
for opportunities to serve in your realm,
and for your Spirit,
empowering us to live a life worthy of our calling.
Root and establish us in love,
that, with all God's people, we may have power
to comprehend the deep meaning of our life in Christ.
Strengthen us in faith
that we may know the love of Christ,
even though it is beyond knowledge,
and so be filled with all the fullness of God;
through Jesus Christ our Lord. Amen.[2]

CONCERNS OF THE CHURCH

Here worshippers are invited to voice their joys, concerns, invitations to community action, prayer requests, etc.

SONG

"I Was There to Hear Your Borning Cry," text and tune
by John Ylvisaker (see above p. 22 for words)[3]

HEARING THE WORD

Romans 8:12–17
John 3:1–17

REFLECTING ON THE WORD:
Trusting Each Other to the Wind

Today we celebrate not only that a child was born, but that she is born
anew; and we share a commitment to her ongoing rebirth. In this way,
we are "writing the check" — with the ongoing prayer that she will
one day endorse it herself.

In every other way, her baptism is for *us*. She won't know or remember what we are doing here; but *we* will remember once more how
we are all connected, as we repeat an ancient practice of the church
by asking this tiny candidate for baptism, "What is your name?" This
morning the whole congregation will answer for her, "Madelyn Claire."

Jesus reminds us that baptism is about water, a visible sign, and the
Spirit — an invisible life and calling from God. And then, in words the
church has too long neglected as a mere passing statement, he adds,
"The wind blows where it will. . . . You don't know whence it comes or
where it is going; and so it is with everyone who is born of the Spirit!"

"The unknown will dance away from you toward the horizon of
light," writes the poet Wendell Berry; and we know the one born of
the Spirit will be dancing there, too — out of our reach. It has been
said that mystics are ungovernable. It would seem that anyone born
of the Spirit is *profoundly* ungovernable. We must remember that this
child's heart, finally, is not ours to govern.

This says something about the way we will *keep* our promise to
nurture her — not with rigid dogma, but with trust for the breath of
God and a tender respect for *her* spirit.

One of the most subtle and poignant moments in an infant baptism
is when the parents give the child up by handing her to the minister,
symbolically handing her to the whole church. She will never again be
just *their* child. And so, in this act of great courage, this letting go,
we trust her to the holy wind that is the Spirit of the living God. She
will be at once *alone* there in divine hands, and *surrounded* by a great
cloud of witnesses.

As we say loudly, "My name is Madelyn Claire," let us be reminded
that if we entrust one so little to that mighty power, then we can also

entrust each other to the same Wind — with the same trust, and the same tender respect.

— Gail A. Ricciuti

QUIET REFLECTION

During these moments, a suggested musical interlude is "The Circle Game," by Joni Mitchell[4]

THE SACRAMENT OF BAPTISM FOR MADELYN CLAIRE BROWN

READING

In the great circle,
dancing in and out of time,
you move now toward your partners,
answering the music suddenly audible to you
that only carried you before
and will carry you again.
When you meet the destined ones now dancing toward you,
we will be in line behind you,
out of your awareness for the time,
we whom you know,
others we remember whom you do not remember,
others forgotten by us all.
When you meet, and hold love in your arms,
regardless of all,
the unknown will dance away from you toward the horizon of light.
Our names will flutter on these hills like little fires.[5]

PRAYERS OVER THE WATER

The bowl containing the water for baptism is passed around the circle, from person to person. Each worshipper who wishes to voice prayers or hopes for the significance of baptismal waters in the child's life is invited to do so while holding the bowl in his or her hands.

THE BAPTISMAL PROMISES

Here the baptismal promises of a community's own faith tradition may be used.

- by the parents

- by the community

THE BAPTISM

Minister: What is your name?

People: Madelyn Claire.

After the child is baptized, the minister and community join in this blessing:

All: Madelyn Claire, child of the covenant,
may you grow into a strong woman of faith!

REMEMBERING OUR OWN BAPTISM

God of life and goodness, we praise you for claiming us
through our baptism; and we remember your promises.
Lord, uphold us by your Holy Spirit.
Daily increase in us your gifts of grace:
the spirit of wisdom and understanding,
the spirit of counsel and might,
the spirit of knowledge and reverence for you,
the spirit of joy in your presence,
both now and forever. Amen.

— Adapted from *Holy Baptism and
Services for the Renewal of Baptism*

PASSING THE PEACE

Participants are invited to greet each other with the words:

The promises of God are for you.

SONG

Water Has Held Us[6]
tune: "Morning Has Broken"

Water has held us, moved by creation.
Out of dark chaos, broke forth the light.
Up from the deluge, showing God's promise
Has come a rainbow, gladdening sight.

Water has saved us, as the sea parted
For Israel's children, walled on each side.
This love has led us, helped us in trouble;
On far horizon, God's cloud our guide.

Water has cleansed us, bathed with forgiveness
Has, with clear blessing, washed sin away.
Jordan's strong currents, God's Own announcing,
Made a beginning, baptismal day.

> Water has touched us, fresh on our foreheads,
> Showing an inward, spiritual grace.
> Into God's family, we have been welcomed:
> As sons and daughters, we take our place.

BENEDICTION

RESPONSE

"Come, Spirit" (Reprise)

•

SUGGESTED ALTERNATE HYMNS

"Child of Blessing, Child of Promise" (TPH, UMH)

"Down to Earth, As a Dove" (TPH)

"God of the Sparrow" (TPH, UMH)

NOTES

1. The invocation "Come, Spirit" is from *WomanPrayer, WomanSong*, by Miriam Therese Winter, Meyer-Stone Books, 1987.

2. The Prayer of Thanks is reprinted from *Holy Baptism and Services for the Renewal of Baptism: The Worship of God* (Supplemental Liturgical Resource 2). © 1985, Westminster Press. Used by permission of Westminster/John Knox Press.

3. "I Was There to Hear Your Borning Cry," words and music by John Ylvisaker. Used by permission. © 1985 John Ylvisaker, Box 321, Waverly, IA 50677.

4. "The Circle Game," from "Joni Mitchell Anthology," Warner Brothers 265 Secaucus Rd., Secaucus, NJ 07096.

5. "Our Children, Coming of Age," excerpted from *Collected Poems*, © 1984 by Wendell Berry. Published by North Point Press and reprinted by permission.

6. The words to "Water Has Held Us" © 1980 Christian Century Foundation. Reprinted by permission from the November 1980 issue of *The Christian Ministry*.

18

THE MASK OF THE PHARISEE
(Ordinary Time/Reformation)

INTRODUCTION

Those who follow the discipline of a weekly lectionary to anchor worship often discover, as we have, that the Holy Spirit molds and moves within such cycles far beyond anything official lectionary committees may expect. When the Common Lectionary presented us with the parable of the Pharisee and the tax collector on Reformation Sunday — just before Halloween — we were struck with what playfulness and grace Dame Wisdom had shown once again.

This parable presents two of the most poignant and intriguing characterizations of the human condition in all of Jesus' teachings. However, to experience its true impact we must first divest ourselves of some "churchy" stereotypes. John Dominic Crossan, in his book *The Dark Interval: Towards a Theology of Story*, points out that centuries of rather nasty and inaccurate Christian polemics against the Pharisees stand in the way of the parable's true mission — which, like all parables, is to overturn our expectation and thereby challenge the security of our self-made world.[1] The original hearers of Jesus' tale revered the Pharisee as a moral leader, while we immediately hear the title "Pharisee" to imply "villain." As a result, our structure of expectation is left unthreatened by the story; so that it is apt to leave us emotionally cold. Such a jaded understanding raises hermeneutical questions: How to recover the "whack on the head" such a parable should achieve? How to recognize the almost humorous contrast between the one able to delude himself about his moral uprightness because he is a "good citizen," and the other who *knows* himself to be of a despised group of notoriously questionable morality!

The posturing of the Pharisee in Jesus' parable suggests the self-aggrandizement of a person hiding behind a mask of piety. But it seems

132

that this model citizen believes what he is saying. He does not put *on* a mask: it is the mask he doesn't notice over his own face, which blurs his perception, both of himself and his distant brother, the tax collector. Each one of us metaphorically harbors both a Pharisee and a tax collector, the one who prays "thus with himself" (as if to suggest admiring glances in a mirror rather than God-ward) and the one who chooses not to hide from self or from God and can only rely on divine mercy. It is in fact one of the great themes of the Reformation that "by grace you are saved, through faith" (Rom. 5:1–2) — that none of us can earn (*either* through effort or accomplishment) the astonishing love of God.

PREPARATION

In a season when masks are so readily available (specifically the half-masks traditionally worn for costume balls), worshippers are invited to "act out" their spiritual identification with both characters by worshipping first for a time "with masks on," and then to experience the heart-transforming grace of God as we gently remove one another's masks.

Participants are seated in a large circle with a table in the center. An old galvanized metal garbage can stands nearby. Before the service, a half-mask is placed on each chair. Worship begins with a narrator and two "players" reading the Lucan story in a simple tableau: The "Pharisee," wearing a fancier feathered mask, speaks while gazing at himself/herself adoringly in a hand mirror (to which is taped a copy of the text). The "tax collector" is kneeling some distance away, outside the circle, with his/her back to the participants. At the appropriate time in the reading, he/she cries out in supplication, "God, be merciful to me, a sinner!"

•

GATHERING, WE HEAR THE STORY

Luke 18:9–14

When the reading is finished, a worship leader invites participants to join in the Response and then to put on the masks.

Response: God, I thank you that I am not like other people!

HYMN OF CELEBRATION

Who Is on the Lord's Side?[2]

Who is on the Lord's side? Who will serve the King?
Who will be His helpers, Other lives to bring?

Who will leave the world's side? Who will face the foe?
Who is on the Lord's side? Who for Him will go?
By Thy call of mercy, By Thy grace divine,
We are on the Lord's side, Saviour we are Thine.

Fierce may be the conflict, Strong may be the foe,
But the King's own army None can overthrow:
Round His standard ranging, Victory is secure;
For His truth unchanging Makes the triumph sure.
Joyfully enlisting By Thy grace divine,
We are on the Lord's side, Saviour, we are Thine.

—Frances Ridley Havergal,
The Hymnal (1933)

CONFESSING WHO WE ARE

A leader invites participants to picture silently, in their mind's eye, their answers to each of the following questions, and after each question, to join in the printed response:

- What do you secretly believe makes you a little bit superior to other people?
- What is your pet peeve in other people?
- What do you feel is your most commendable quality?
- What do you judge to be the biggest cowardice in others?

    Response: God, I thank you that I am not like other people!

OFFERING DEDICATION

Participants are asked to come forward and place their offerings in a silver bowl on the table.

    Unison: Here — let me help you, Lord:

    I am happy to pledge a healthy sum to advance your rule.

    Let my money bring the unjust, the evil, the immoral, and the lazy to Christ; and so make this world a better place.

    Feel free to call on me any time I can be of assistance to your cause. Alleluia, and amen!

Choral Response (reprise of hymn chorus):

    By Thy call of mercy, By Thy grace divine,
    We are on the Lord's side, Saviour, we are Thine!

TIME FOR CONTENTED REFLECTION

Suggested music for reflection:
"With God on Our Side," by Bob Dylan[3]

LISTENING FOR THE WORD

The Room of Righteous Indignation

The guestmaster looked at me carefully and lead me to a room marked "Righteous Indignation."

"Good," I thought, "back home some people don't understand me. They think I'm judgmental. But this man understands."

There wasn't much in the room besides the four walls, and that was all right with me. I sat down and meditated a while. Then I read my Bible. I found myself looking at those walls. I read some more, then meditated, then looked at the walls again. Late in the evening, as I was staring at one of the walls, it became transparent, and I found myself looking at my own monastery. Fascinating. What's more, as I watched, I found I could see right through its walls and into its church and cloisters.

After a while I could even see inside the cell of each monk. I saw everything. I saw what each monk had in his room and what he was doing. I saw some praying, some sleeping, some reading. I could even see what each one was reading. Brother! Do you see what that one is reading? And look at the private property! Soon I could hear their voices. I could hear everything that was said — the complaints, the backbiting. My own name was mentioned. Huh — that one to be complaining of me!

I began to take notes. I filled page after page. I had thought the place was bad before, but here were the facts — what they said, what they did, what they had. Nothing subjective — just cold facts. As I kept writing, I began to see right into their heads, to see their very thoughts. These I also wrote down.

Once, when I was resting my eyes, the thought came to me, "I wonder what I would see if the other wall were transparent? Perhaps if I kept looking at it long enough. . . . Well, it did open up and through it I saw the Magic Monastery, every bit of it. What an eyeful! I thought my own place was bad. Talk about individualism. I began to write that down too.

I rang for the Brother and asked him to bring me some more notebooks. There was so much to get down. From time to time a further question would come to me, "I wonder what's behind these other two walls?" I became uncomfortable. "Who is there? What are the walls hiding? Why don't they let me see? It's probably dreadful." I took to staring at these walls. The Brother said that behind the one wall were the deceased members of the Magic Monastery, and behind the other were the deceased members of my own monastery.

"Ah," I said, "but why can't I see them? I want to see them."

"You won't like it," he said.

"Truth, that's all I want. That's all I've ever wanted. I call a spade a spade. Show me!"

"You'll only get angry."

"Show me. Bring me some more notebooks, and show me."

But he refused and hurried away. I was determined that when he returned the next day I would get the truth out of him.

I did. I took him by the throat and demanded to know what was going on behind those walls. "Behind this one," he gasped, "are the deceased members of your own community. They are all looking in at you. They are weeping and praying for you.

"Behind this other wall are all the deceased members of the Magic Monastery. They are all looking at you and laughing."

—Theophane the Monk,
Tales of a Magic Monastery[4]

The reading is followed by a brief period of silence.

CONFESSING WHO WE REALLY ARE

The leader again asks participants to picture each answer in their minds, followed in each case by the unison response:

- Recall again what you secretly believe makes you superior to others.

- Recall your judgment about the greatest cowardice in other people.

- What gift in yourself have you neglected or allowed to lie fallow?

- Recall the most recent occasion when you cut yourself off from the support of the community.

    Response: God, be merciful to me, a sinner!

REDEEMING THE PHARISEE WITHIN

Participants are invited to stand. The leader goes to one person in the circle, removes that person's mask, and says to him/her the response, "I tell you, this one went home justified rather than the other...." The leader drops the mask into the garbage can and returns to her/his place in the circle. The person who has just been "unmasked" goes in turn to someone else, and so on until all have had their masks removed.

    Response: I tell you, this one went home justified rather than the
                other....

THE SONG OF THE REDEEMED

Somebody Touched Me[5]
Spiritual

1. Somebody touched me when I was praying
   Somebody touched me when I was praying
   Somebody touched me when I was praying
   It must have been the hand of the Lord.

2. Somebody touched me when I was calling
   Somebody touched me when I was calling
   Somebody touched me when I was calling
   It must have been the hand of the Lord.

3. Somebody touched me when I was seeking
   Somebody touched me when I was seeking
   Somebody touched me when I was seeking
   It must have been the hand of the Lord.

4. Somebody touched me when I was singing
   Somebody touched me when I was singing
   Somebody touched me when I was singing
   It must have been the hand of the Lord.

OFFERING DEDICATION (unison)

All that we have, all that we are, all that we are to be can never repay
the love-debt we owe; and so with grateful hearts, our God, we return
your own to you. Amen.

SONG

Lord I Want to Be a Christian
Spiritual

1. Lord I want to be a Christian in-a my heart, in-a my heart;
   Lord I want to be a Christian in-a my heart.
   In-a my heart, in-a my heart,
   Lord I want to be a Christian in-a my heart.

2. Lord, I want to be more loving....

3. Lord, I want to be more holy....

4. Lord, I want to be like Jesus....

PRAYER

Voice: This tax collector seemed to know precisely who he was, "a sinner." Simply that. He didn't make excuses, compare himself with other persons more outrageous than himself, didn't even offer up the occasional generous impulse in an attempt to balance his offenses. He admitted who he was, then asked God's mercy, and he got it.

Unison: Bring me, Lord, to such honesty.

Let me know myself as I am known within your holy presence.

Then may I find myself both humbled and restored, not in public acts of fasting, tithing, and the like, but by the steady, quiet transformation that your Holy Spirit works in those who trust in you. Amen.

—adapted from a selection in
A Diary of Prayer, J. Barrie Shepherd[6]

THE BLESSING

SONG

"God Be with You Till We Meet Again"; tune: Randolph; *The Presbyterian Hymnal*, United Methodist Hymnal

•

NOTES

1. John Dominic Crossan, *The Dark Interval: Towards a Theology of Story* (Allen, Tex.: Argus Communications, 1975).

2. "Who Is on the Lord's Side?" (a hymn in the public domain). The tune and words from *The Hymnal* (Philadelphia: Presbyterian Board of Christian Education, 1933).

3. "With God on Our Side" words and music by Bob Dylan. Produced by Warner Bros. Publications, 265 Secaucus Rd. Secaucus, NJ 07094.

4. "The Room of Righteous Indignation," from *Tales of a Magic Monastery* by Theophane the Monk (New York: Crossroad, 1988).

5. "Somebody Touched Me" and "Lord, I Want to Be a Christian," words and music can be found in *Folk Encounter*. Both songs are in the public domain.

6. The prayer "Bring Me, Lord, to Such Honesty..." is adapted from *A Diary of Prayer: Meditations on the Parables of Jesus*, by J. Barrie Shepherd, © 1981 Westminster Press. Used by permission of Westminster/John Knox Press.

19

THE JONAH IN US

(Ordinary Time/
Despair and Deliverance)

INTRODUCTION

It is a paradox experienced by many people of faith: the longer one lives and the deeper one moves into true spirituality, the less certainty one has about things that formerly appeared obvious. And one begins to understand that the inspiration of Scripture has more to do with the *questions* it asks than with the answers it contains. The story of Jonah is just such a masterpiece. In the space of four short chapters, it challenges our cherished assumptions about sin and repentance, God's purposes and our own motivations, and the meaning of grace.

In the midst of these serious questions we meet the refreshingly salty Jonah, another of the Bible's unlikely candidates to be singled out by God for a life-and-death evangelistic mission! The man does not want the job. When called by the insistent word of the Lord to arise and go to Nineveh, he arises, all right! — but in order to find a ship heading the other way. Nevertheless, Jonah is a character with a conscience, honestly offering a self-incriminating explanation for the fierce storm that batters that ship. His subsequent adventure is authentic to human experience, a metaphor that speaks volumes to anyone who has ever been cast into the belly of a Leviathan-sized distress.

Yet while the story offers us possibilities for somber reflection, Jonah is also a comical figure — precisely because he mirrors *our* most amusing foibles in encountering God. It is not always "godspel," good news, to know of God's mercy toward those *we* consider worthy only of a good, swift kick. Here is portrayed an Almighty who "repents" in response to repentance, not the rigid God of retribution who would be so much more to our liking. Jonah is swift to justify his initial resistance to God's call by angrily *accusing* God for having grace, mercy, patience, and steadfast love. It is too much to swallow for anyone with a modicum of *principle*; and Jonah takes his indignation and stomps off to sit in the shade and pout.

The last word — the last laugh, really — is had by this God who, in addition to the horribly wonderful qualities that have so angered Jonah, also possesses a sense of humor. After staging a final drama-within-a-drama as an object lesson for the recalcitrant prophet, the Holy asks whether there should not be divine pity for that great city "in which there are more than 120,000 persons who do not know their right hand from their left, and also much cattle?" Few books in the canon end so abruptly, with what the poet Anne Sexton called "that untamable, eternal, gut-driven *ha-ha*."

Entering into Jonah's story in worship can be proof that our tears and our laughter truly are inseparable, and that together, they open the door to self-recognition, to repentance, to forgiveness of others, and thus to God's amazing grace.

PREPARATION

This service treats the entire story of the book of Jonah as one seamless piece, rather than lifting out a fragmented "text" for the day. In this context, the worship experience that emerges from the story is a "pageant" in which the people move from place to place and experience the story liturgically. For this purpose, it is necessary to print portions of the biblical text in the order of worship so that dramatic parts can be assigned to various voices.

Many churches have unused storage, cellar, or attic spaces, dark and forgotten, that provide wonderful settings in which to create the "belly of the whale." A basement "catacombs" yields a perfect niche where bare light bulbs create an eerie, blood-colored glow through bolts of red fabric draped from low ceilings; voices become muffled acoustically, and just enough dim light for reading is provided. The descent down cellar stairs and through dusty passageways sets the mood for this experience of being "swallowed" in the belly of the church(!), yielding unexpected meanings that both children and adults will discuss long afterward.

•

CHAPTER ONE

PRELUDE

"I Come Tired," Richard Avery and Donald Marsh,
Songs for the Search[1]

ENTERING THE STORY

Any portions not assigned to specific voices are read by one narrator. Other voices are recruited in advance from among the worshippers. In the case of the group of sailors, for instance, the entire community is invited to read.

Jonah 1:1-7:

Now the word of the Lord came to Jonah the son of Amittai, saying,

> *God:* Arise, go to Nineveh, that great city, and cry against it; for their wickedness has come up before me.

But Jonah rose to flee to Tarshish from the presence of the Lord. He went down to Joppa and found a ship going to Tarshish; so he paid the fare, and went on board, to go with them to Tarshish, away from the presence of the Lord.

But the Lord hurled a great wind upon the sea, and there was a mighty tempest on the sea, so that the ship threatened to break up. Then the mariners were afraid, and each cried to his god; and they threw the wares that were in the ship into the sea, to lighten it for them. But Jonah had gone down into the inner part of the ship and had lain down, and was fast asleep. So the captain came and said to him,

> *Captain:* What do you mean, you sleeper? Arise, call upon your god! Perhaps the god will give a thought to us, that we do not perish.

And they said to one another,

> *Sailors:* Come, let us cast lots, that we may know on whose account this evil has come upon us.

So they cast lots, and the lot fell upon Jonah.

SONG

Jonah[2]

> We sail a ship with a man named Jonah,
> We sail a ship with a man named Jonah,
> We sail a ship with a man named Jonah,
> earlye in the morning.

Chorus:
Lord, our God, have mercy on us,
Lord, our God, have mercy on us,
Lord, our God, have mercy on us,
earlye in the morning.

    2. Fall on your knees, for the sea is raging.
    3. Who is the guilty one among us?
    4. Cast the lot, and the number's Jonah's.
    5. Row, row, to save this Jonah!
    6. O Lord God, we've got to drown him.
    7. Done, and the sea has ceased its raging.
    8. Lord, send a fish and a resurrection.
    9. What shall we do when the world is drowning?
    10. Lord, send a fish and a resurrection.

Jonah 1:8–13:

Then they said to him,

    Sailors: Tell us, on whose account this evil has come upon us?
                 What is your occupation? And whence do you come?
                 What is your country? And of what people are you?

And he said to them,

    Jonah: I am a Hebrew; and I fear the Lord, the God of heaven,
              who made the sea and the dry land.

Then the men were exceedingly afraid, and said to him,

    Sailors: What is this that you have done!

For the men knew that he was fleeing from the presence of the Lord, because he had told them. Then they said to him,

    Sailors: What shall we do to you, that the sea may quiet down
              for us?

For the sea grew more and more tempestuous. He said to them,

    Jonah: Take me up and throw me into the sea; then the sea
              will quiet down for you; for I know it is because of me
              that this great tempest has come upon you.

Nevertheless the men rowed hard to bring the ship back to land, but they could not, for the sea grew more and more tempestuous against them.

POEM

Read by a worshipper, preferably a poet!

Rowing
by Anne Sexton[3]

A story, a story!
(Let it go. Let it come.)
I was stamped out like a Plymouth fender
into this world.
First came the crib
with its glacial bars.
Then dolls
and the devotion to their plastic mouths.
Then there was school,
the little straight rows of chairs,
blotting my name over and over,
but undersea all the time,
a stranger whose elbows wouldn't work.
Then there was life
with its cruel houses
and people who seldom touched —
though touch is all —
but I grew,
like a pig in a trenchcoat I grew,
and then there were many strange apparitions,
the nagging rain, the sun turning into poison
and all of that, saws working through my heart,
but I grew, I grew,
and God was there like an island I had not rowed to,
still ignorant of Him, my arms and my legs worked,
and I grew, I grew,
I wore rubies and bought tomatoes
and now, in my middle age,
about nineteen in the head I'd say,
I am rowing, I am rowing,
though the oarlocks stick and are rusty
and the sea blinks and rolls
like a worried eyeball, but I am rowing, I am rowing,
though the wind pushes me back
and I know that island will not be perfect,
it will have the flaws of life,
the absurdities of the dinner table,
but there will be a door
and I will open it
and I will get rid of the rat inside of me,
the gnawing pestilential rat.

God will take it with his two hands
and embrace it.

As the African says:
This is my tale which I have told,
if it be sweet, if it be not sweet,
take somewhere else and let some return to me.
This story ends with me still rowing.

Jonah 1:14–17:

Therefore they cried to the Lord,

> *Sailors:*   We beseech thee, O Lord, let us not perish for this
> man's life, and lay not on us innocent blood; for thou,
> O Lord, hast done as it please thee.

So they took up Jonah and threw him into the sea; and the sea ceased
from its raging. Then the men feared the Lord exceedingly, and they
offered a sacrifice to the Lord and made vows. And the Lord appointed
a great fish to swallow up Jonah; and Jonah was in the belly of the fish
three days and three nights.

*Here worshippers are invited to descend into the belly of the "great fish,"
following signs posted along the route through the church. Our signs were
copies of old woodcuts and other artistic renderings of Jonah and the whale,
as well as prints and photos of whales in their natural habitat. The procession
should be undertaken in meditative silence.*

CHAPTER TWO
In the Belly of a Whale

CORPORATE PRAYERS OF CONFESSION

*Worshippers are invited to reflect in silence on the following questions, and
then to voice their answers aloud if they feel moved to do so:*

- Was there a time in your life when God was calling you and you
  ran away?

- Was there ever a time when *anyone* was calling and you ran away?

- Where in this *community* do we run away from God's leading?

LITANY

The Prayer of Jonah: Jonah 2:1–7

> Side 1:   I called to the Lord, out of my distress,
> and God answered me;

Side 2: Out of the belly of Sheol I cried,
and thou didst hear my voice.

Side 1: For thou didst cast me into the deep,
into the heart of the seas,

Side 2: And the flood was round about me;
all thy waves and thy billows passed over me.

SINGING: Jesus, lover of my soul,
let me to thy bosom fly,
while the nearer waters roll,
while the tempest still is high:
hide me, o my savior, hide,
till the storm of life is past;
safe into the haven guide;
O receive my soul at last![4]

Side 1: Then I said, "I am cast out from thy presence;
how shall I again look upon thy holy temple?"

Side 2: The waters closed in over me,
the deep was round about me;
weeds were wrapped about my head
at the roots of the mountains.

Side 1: I went down to the land
whose bars closed upon me for ever....

SINGING: Other refuge have I none;
hangs my helpless soul on thee;
leave, ah! leave me not alone,
still support and comfort me.
all my trust on thee is stayed,
all my help from thee I bring;
cover my defenseless head
with the shadow of thy wing.

All: Yet thou didst bring up my life from the pit,
O Lord my God.
When my soul fainted within me,
I remembered the Lord:
and my prayer came to thee,
into thy holy temple.

At this point in the service, as they leave the "belly of the whale," worshippers are invited to place their offerings in baskets. A quick-witted retiree in our group, Selden, spontaneously announced: "If you want to get out of the whale, cough up!"

CHAPTER THREE
Nineveh Repents, God Repents, and Jonah Gets Mad

PACING OUT THE STORY: Jonah 3:1–5, 10, 4:1–5
The words of Jonah are paraphrased here in modern terms.

Then the word of the Lord came to Jonah the second time, saying,

> *God:* Arise, go to Nineveh, that great city, and proclaim to it the message that I tell you.

So Jonah arose and went to Nineveh, according to the word of the Lord. Now Nineveh was an exceedingly great city, three day's journey in breadth. Jonah began to go into the city, going a day's journey. And he cried,

> *Jonah:* Listen, people: You've got forty days. After that, you're *history!*

And the people of Nineveh believed God; they proclaimed a fast, and put on sackcloth, from the greatest of them to the least of them.... When God saw what they did, how they turned from their evil way, God repented of the evil which he said he would do to them; and he did not do it.
    But it displeased Jonah exceedingly, and he was angry. And he prayed to the Lord and said,

> *Jonah:* I *ask* you, God: isn't this what I predicted back home? That's why I was in a hurry to run away; because I *knew* you were a softie at heart! You have too much *patience!* So go ahead — kill me off. Maybe I'd *rather* be dead!

And the Lord said,

> *God:* Do you do well to be angry?

Then Jonah went out of the city and sat to the east of the city, and made a booth for himself there. He sat under it in the shade, till he should see what would become of the city.

If large potted trees or plants can be procured to set around the worship space, participants may be invited to sit on the floor under them for the remainder of the service.

FINALE
Sulking under a Tree

OVERHEARING THE DISCUSSION: Jonah 4:6–11

And the Lord God appointed a plant, and made it come up over Jonah, that it might be a shade over his head, to save him from his discomfort. So Jonah was exceedingly glad because of the plant. But when dawn came up the next day, God appointed a worm which attacked the plant, so that it withered. When the sun rose, God appointed a sultry east wind, and the sun beat upon the head of Jonah so that he was faint; and he asked that he might die, and said,

Jonah: Maybe I'd *rather* be dead!

But God said to Jonah,

God: Do you do well to be angry for the plant?

Jonah: Yeah, it's okay for me to be mad: mad enough to *croak!*

God: You pity the plant, for which you did not labor, nor did you make it grow, which came into being in a night, and perished in a night. And should not I pity Nineveh, that great city, in which there are more than a hundred and twenty thousand persons who do not know their right hand from their left, and also much cattle?

POEM

The Rowing Endeth

I'm mooring my rowboat
at the dock of the island called God.
This dock is made in the shape of a fish
and there are many boats moored
at many different docks.
"It's okay," I say to myself,
with blisters that broke and healed
and broke and healed —
saving themselves over and over.
And salt sticking to my face and arms like
a glue-skin pocked with grains of tapioca.
I empty myself from my wooden boat
and onto the flesh of The Island.

"On with it!" He says and thus
we squat on the rocks by the sea

and play — can it be true —
a game of poker.
He calls me.
I win because I hold a royal straight flush.
He wins because He holds five aces.
A wild card had been announced
but I had not heard it
being in such a state of awe
when He took out the cards and dealt.
As He plunks down His five aces
and I sit grinning at my royal flush,
He starts to laugh,
the laughter rolling like a hoop out of His mouth
and into mine,
and such laughter that He doubles right over me
laughing a Rejoice-Chorus at our two triumphs.
Then I laugh, the fishy dock laughs
the sea laughs. The Island laughs.
The Absurd laughs.

Dearest dealer,
I with my royal straight flush
love you so for your wild card,
that untamable, eternal, gut-driven *ha-ha*
and lucky love.

— Anne Sexton

SINGING OUR PRAYER

Help Us Accept Each Other

Help us accept each other as Christ accepted us;
teach us as sister, brother each person to embrace.
Be present, Lord, among us and bring us to believe
we are *ourselves* accepted and meant to love and live.

Teach us, O Lord, your lessons, as in our daily life
we struggle to be human and search for hope and faith.
Teach us to care for people, for all — not just for some,
to love them as we find them or as they may become.

Let your acceptance change us, so that we may be moved
in living situations to do the truth in love;
to practice your acceptance until we know by heart
the table of forgiveness and laughter's healing art.

Lord, for today's encounters with all who are in need,
who hunger for acceptance, for righteousness and bread,
we need new eyes for seeing, new hands for holding on:
renew us with your Spirit; Lord, free us, make us one!

— Fred Kaan, *Creation Sings*[5]

BENEDICTION AND POSTSCRIPT

For I know the plans I have for you, says the Lord,
plans for *shalom* and not for evil,
to give you a future and a hope.

— Jeremiah 29:11

•

SUGGESTED ALTERNATE HYMNS

"God of the Sparrow" (TPH, UMH)

"Jesus, Savior, Pilot Me (UMH, HB, PH)

"Lonely the Boat" ("Kahm Kahm hahn Bom Sanaoon") (TPH, UMH)

NOTES

1. "I Come Tired," by Richard Avery and Donald Marsh, from *Songs for the Search: A Portfolio of Songs and Ideas for Presentation*, published by Proclamation Productions, Inc. Orange Square, Port Jervis, NY 12771.

2. "Jonah," words by Ewald Bash to a traditional folk tune. Used by permission of author.

3. "Rowing" and "The Rowing Endeth," from *The Awful Rowing toward God*, by Anne Sexton. Copyright © 1975 by Loring Conant, Jr., executor of the estate of Anne Sexton. Reprinted by permission of Houghton Mifflin Co.

4. "Jesus, Lover of My Soul." Tune: Martyn, from *The Hymnbook*

5. "Help Us Accept Each Other," in *Creation Sings*, words by Fred Kaan and music by Doreen Potter. © 1975 by Hope Publishing Co., Carol Stream, IL 60188. All rights reserved. Used by permission.

20

CATCHING A GLIMPSE OF GOD'S BUSINESS

(Ordinary Time)

INTRODUCTION

This service is intended for the season whose name really describes most of life: just a bit "ordinary." *But* on occasion we catch sight of something truly exciting and life-giving. Those little glimpses make life worth living, or help us to make it through the day. With a glimpse of what God intends for a life, a "direction of travel" may be confirmed. Everyone has examples of such glimpses, but we rarely find the opportunity to talk about them (or think they are too silly to mention). Yet they are crucial to our sense of well-being. In the story of forty years of wilderness wandering, Moses is given only God's promise of a land of milk and honey. Finally, God gives Moses just a glimpse of the "promised land"; and Moses dies. But for that short time Moses sees with his own eyes what God is doing, and, perhaps, Moses is able to die knowing that his life has been worthwhile.

As important as it is to glimpse what God intends for our lives, it is interesting to contemplate the idea that each of us, if we claim the name "Christian," becomes a glimpse of God's handiwork to others. Who we are is an image of what God is about. We are God's wonderful creation and partners in the redemption of creation. We become part of the promise for others. Usually, though, we lose sight of that, caught up in (or overwhelmed by) the "day-to-day" of our lives. We need experiences that put us in touch again with our role in God's creation.

PREPARATION

For this service the worship leader will need to collect business cards from a variety of professions. As the idea of being a glimpse of "God's business" is discussed, the cards are used as visual aids.

The service was originally prepared for an intergenerational group as closing worship for a weekend retreat. Therefore it is designed with the understanding that both children and adults will be full participants.

•

GATHERING

Leader: Praise God!

People: We praise the name of God!

Leader: Give praise, O servants of God!
You stand in the house of the Lord,
in the courts of the house of God!

People: Praise God for God is good.
We sing to God's name
for our God is the gracious one!

SONG

"Joyful, Joyful, We Adore Thee," *The Worshipbook*

WE CONFESS OUR SIN TO GOD (unison)

O God, we confess that we are people who lose our way at times.
Our footsteps falter, our eyes turn away,
and we are preoccupied with our own needs and concerns.
Even our love for one another grows cold.

We trust in your grace to create new life within us.
We trust in your love to bind us together as a family of faith.
Let your spirit be born in us. Again.
Accept us this day, for Christ's sake.
Amen.

ASSURANCE OF PARDON

THE PEACE

Leader: This is God's house, a place of peace:
a place where we befriend one another
in the name of Christ.

People: We enter strangers.
We leave as friends.

Leader: Let us greet one another as a sign of God's peace
and Christ's friendship.
May the peace of Christ be with each of you.

People: And also with you.

— Rosemary C. Mitchell

WE HEAR THE WORD OF GOD

Deuteronomy 34:1–12

INTERPRETING THE WORD OF GOD:
"Catching a Glimpse of God's Business"
(Reflection by worship leader)

In this passage Moses receives a glimpse of the Promised Land, a
glimpse of what God is about, a glimpse of God's "business." Just
a glimpse; then Moses dies.

When we claim the name "Christian," can we say that we have a
glimpse of God's business? In our words and acts of love, peace, and
justice, do we share with others a glimpse of God's business? Do we
ourselves become a sign for others? Have you ever thought of yourself
that way?

God intends *us* to be that glimpse of what is promised.

Many people carry business cards. The purpose of a business card is
to give some information and a glimpse of what one does for a living.

*At this point the worship leader shows the group the various samples of
business cards and passes them around so that people can see them up close.
Each participant is given a 5" x 8" index card and instructed to write
his/her name in the center of the card. Each person exchanges the card
with three others in the group. With each exchange people are asked to
write a word or draw a symbol or picture on the card, portraying how its
owner is a glimpse of God's business.*

SMALL GROUP TIME

People are invited to share what they discovered on their card.

SONG

"Open My Eyes," *The Hymnbook*

CLOSING PRAYER

Open our eyes, O God, that we may see your vision of the realm of
heaven. In seeing we may also become a glimpse of that vision, a sign
for others of what you intend for all creation. We give thanks for the

life of Jesus Christ, that by his life we have more than a glimpse of who you are and what you intend for our lives. We give thanks for those people in our lives who have been a glimpse of your love and hope. May we continue to grow to be signs for others in this world. Amen.

SONG

"We Plow the Fields and Scatter," *The Hymnbook*

BLESSING

•

SUGGESTED ALTERNATE HYMNS

"All Beautiful the March of Days" (vs. 1, 3) (TPH, WB, HB, PH)

"Arise, Your Light Is Come!" (TPH)

"Be Thou My Vision" (TPH, UMH, WB, HB, PH)

"Come, O Thou God of Grace" (WB)

"Cuando el Pobre" (When a Poor One) (TPH, UMH)

"From All That Dwell Below the Skies" (TPH, UMH, WB, HB, PH)

"God of Grace, God of Glory" (TPH, UMH, WB, HB, PH)

"God of Our Life through All the Circling Years" (WB, PH, HB)

"Immortal Invisible" (vs. 1, 2, 3,) (TPH, UMH, WB, PH, HB)

"Joyful, Joyful" (vs. 1, 2, 3,) (TPH, UMH, WB, HB, PH)

"Let There Be Light" (vs. 1, 2, 4,) (UMH, WB, HB, PH)

"O God the Creator" (TPH)

"O Grant Us Light That We May Know" (HB)

"Take Thou Our Minds" (TPH, WB, HB)

21

ANOINTING
(Ordinary Time)

INTRODUCTION

"So strange / so sweet / so shocking / so absurd," writes Thomas John Carlisle in his poem "Justification": "The rhyme and reason / of her reckless gift / have no excuse / but love."[1]

A wealthy woman enters the dining room carrying an alabaster jar and in a startling, timeless motion breaks it open. The costliest, the sweetest, the most aromatic nard pours out like honey — or like lifeblood — over the feet of this man marked for death. In this moment, she expresses a breath-stopping kind of ecstasy* in pouring out her dowry — that which passes from mother to daughter to granddaughter, giving each their identity and their means. She empties herself and becomes poor like him, in this stunning act of relationship to Jesus. She who once sat at his feet in rapt attentiveness (to her sister's great irritation) now anoints those feet extravagantly — to the great irritation of the "real" disciples.

With a prophetic twist of her hand, Mary the sister of Martha also does what none of the other disciples could bring themselves to do, in accepting and sharing in his impending death. It requires courage to embrace the imminence of another's death. It takes vulnerability to touch the living, let alone the dying, with tenderness. And it takes *ecstasy* to move out of the static place of fear into this act of honest compassion.

Ironically, our suspicion of her passionate, spendthrift action has led us to assume what the Gospel does not say: that she must have been hiding some great sin and thus *had* to perform this "penance" in order to "make good." Strange, isn't it, how we interpret generosity and tenderness as a signal of guilt!

---

* *Ek* means "out of" and *stasis* means a state of standstill. Therefore, the one who lives with ecstasy is always exploring *new* aspects of reality, moving away from rigidly fixed situations, leaving the static place.

Within us all, and within our communities, the frugal and restraining voice of Judas will always try to "talk sense" into Mary, standing there with the broken pieces of an alabaster jar in her hands. "The funds are in the bank for a rainy day" will always argue with "The funds are there to be poured out." Middle-class American Christians (with our position of tremendous affluence in the global community) must reckon with the fact that this debate could only happen in *our* churches. The Christian base communities of Latin America, for instance, often pour out from their relative poverty more than we do from our abundance; and they do so without wasting energy or time on such philosophical debates.

Mary of Bethany is an image of what the church is beckoned to replicate, we people of God who have such a spendthrift calling. "The church is called to undertake this mission even at the risk of losing its life...doing those deeds in the world that point beyond themselves to the new reality in Christ."[2] Our sister stands among us in the demeanor of an eccentric and a spendthrift. Yet in her appears the face of a people called forth to announce a new realm, in which "respectable" values will be turned ec-statically upside down.

PREPARATION

The worship is best focused on a stage or presentation area, with participants seated in a semicircle.

A contemporary expression of the anointing of dusty, road-weary feet is the shining of shoes. For that symbolic act, materials should be at hand including shoeshine cloths, some clean shoe brushes for suede, and neutral shoe cleaner/conditioner.

•

GATHERING

SHARING CONCERNS

SONG

"Great Day," African-American Spiritual, *The Presbyterian Hymnal*

THE PRAYERS OF GOD'S PEOPLE:
Psalm 126 (ILL, Year B)[3]

> *All:* When God restored the fortunes of Zion,
> we were like those who dream.

> *Men:* Then our mouth was filled with laughter,
> and our tongue with shouts of joy;

Women: Then they said among the nations,
          "God has done great things for them."

All: God has done great things for us; we are glad.

Women: Restore our fortunes, O God,
          like the watercourses in the Negeb!

Men: May those who sow in tears reap with shouts of joy!

All: Those who go forth weeping,
          bearing the seed for sowing,
          shall come home with shouts of joy,
          bearing their sheaves of grain.

GOD'S RESPONSE:
Isaiah 43:16–21 (ILL, Year C)

All: Thus says the sovereign who makes a way in the sea,
          a path in the mighty waters,
          who brings forth chariot and horse, army and warrior;
          they lie down, they cannot rise,
          they are extinguished, quenched like a wick:

Young Voices: "Remember not the former things,
          nor consider the things of old.
          Behold, I am doing a new thing;
          now it springs forth, do you not perceive it?
          I will make a way in the wilderness
          and rivers in the desert.
          The wild beasts will honor me,
          the jackals and the ostriches;
          for I give water in the wilderness,
          rivers in the desert,
          to give drink to my chosen people,
          the people whom I formed for myself
          that they might declare my praise."

PASSING THE PEACE

HEARING THE WORD

The Gospel: John 12:1–8

It is suggested that the story be dramatically presented by youth, in a contemporary context. The biblical text can be read aloud preceding or following the presentation.

RESPONSE

Judas and Mary[4]

1. Said Judas to Mary, "Now what will you do
   With your ointment so rich and so rare?"
   "I'll pour it all over the feet of the Lord,
   And I'll wipe it away with my hair," she said,
   "I'll wipe it away with my hair."

2. "Oh Mary, oh Mary, oh think of the poor —
   This ointment it could have been sold;
   And think of the blankets and think of the bread
   You could buy with the silver and gold," he said.
   "You could buy with the silver and gold."

3. "Tomorrow, tomorrow I'll think of the poor,
   Tomorrow," she said, "not today
   For dearer than all of the poor of the world
   Is my love who is going away," she said.
   "My love who is going away."

4. Said Jesus to Mary, "Your love is so deep,
   Today you may do as you will.
   Tomorrow, you say, I am going away,
   But my body I leave with you still," he said,
   "My body I leave with you still."

5. "The poor of the world are my body," he said,
   "To the end of the world they shall be;
   The bread and the blankets you give to the poor
   You'll find you have given to me," he said,
   "You'll find you have given to me."

6. "My body will hang on the cross of the world
   Tomorrow," he said, "and today,
   And Martha and Mary will find me again
   And wash all my sorrow away," he said,
   "And wash all my sorrow away."

— Sydney Carter, *In the Present Tense*

REFLECTING ON THE WORD:
"The Outlandish Thing in the World of the Poor"

The worship leader may use ideas found in the Introduction (p. 154) as a basis to reflect upon text and drama.

SONG

"Whatsoever You Do," words and music by Willard F. Jabusch, from *Songbook for Saints and Sinners*[5]

CONFESSING WHO WE ARE (group discussion)

- In what ways do you see Judas and Mary in the life of this community? In yourself?
- How does the Judas treat the Mary in yourself? In the experience of this community?

RESPONSE

> Loving God,
> you know our weakness
> and the extent of our failure
> to love you and one another.
> You see the sincerity of our efforts as well.
> Look upon us who have been offended
> and lift up our hearts.
> Look upon us who have given offense
> and help us heal the hurt we have caused.
> As we willingly,
> with your help,
> forgive one another,
> we ask you to forgive us
> and fill us with your healing power and grace.
> Amen.

— Janet Schaffran and Pat Kozak,
More Than Words[6]

THE SACRAMENT OF FORGIVENESS

Worshippers are invited to choose one person to "anoint" by polishing or brushing his or her shoes. Each partner in turn kneels down (if possible) to "anoint" the other in silence, reflecting on the presence of Christ in him or her, performing the act as if ministering to the Christ. When the task is completed, and before the anointer rises, the one who was anointed is asked to place a hand on her/his head or shoulder and pray silently for that person. Then the two change places and repeat the ritual.

SONG

"A Spendthrift Lover Is the Lord," by Thomas Troeger and Carol Doran, in *New Hymns for the Lectionary*

CHARGE AND BENEDICTION

Anointing

Leader: Anointing has a multiplicity of meaning:
to cool, comfort, heal;
to celebrate with joy;
to prepare for burial;
or to acknowledge a king.
And Christ, the Anointed One,
embraces them all.

— Thomas John Carlisle,
Beginning with Mary[7]

All: May Christ the Anointed One
embrace *us* all,
to heal, celebrate, fortify,
and name us all our days. Amen.

•

SUGGESTED ALTERNATE HYMNS

"Pues Si Vivimos" (When We are Living) (UMH, TPH)

"Standing in the Need of Prayer" (UMH)

NOTES

1. "Justification," by Thomas John Carlisle from *Beginning with Mary*. William B. Eerdmans Publishing Co., Grand Rapids, MI 49503. © 1986. Used by permission of the publisher.

2. Form of Government, Presbyterian Church (USA), G-3.0400.

3. The Inclusive Language Lectionary, Years A, B, and C, published by the Division of Education and Ministry of the National Council of the Churches of Christ, U.S.A., copyright © 1983, 1984, 1985.

4. "Judas and Mary," text and music by Sydney Carter in *Songs of Sydney Carter: In the Present Tense*, vol. 1. Copyright 1964, Galliard, Ltd. Used by permission of Galaxy Music-Boston.

5. "Whatsoever You Do," words and music by Rev. W. F. Jabusch as found in *Songbook for Saints and Sinners*, compiled by Carlton R. Young. Published by Agape, © 1971.

6. The prayer "Loving God..." is from *More Than Words, Prayer and Ritual for Inclusive Communities* by Janet Schaffran and Pat Kozak, Meyer-Stone Books, 1988.

7. "Anointing," by Thomas John Carlisle from *Beginning with Mary*. William B. Eerdmans Publishing Co., Grand Rapids, MI 49503. © 1986. Used by permission of the publisher.

22

WISDOM
(Dedication of Teachers)

INTRODUCTION

The teaching ministry is the backbone of the Reformed tradition. John Calvin regarded teachers as one of the four church offices, in addition to preachers, elders, and deacons. Too often the dedication of teachers is neglected or a mere "add-on" to the worship order when it should be taken as seriously as the ordination of officers. Teaching and passing on our tradition to the next generation is critical to the survival of the faith community, and an important reminder to the congregation.

Christian Education doesn't somehow just happen each week, but requires many hours of planning by dedicated people throughout the year; and recognition of those who volunteer to promote Christian Education contributes to the effectiveness of this ministry. It is also important to know that all we do in the life of a congregation teaches, whether we are intentional or unintentional about our efforts.

Corporate planning of a teacher dedication is especially helpful when a spectrum of ages will be present in worship, since small logistical details can make all the difference in the experience.

The reading "Finding Wisdom" was written to reflect a variety of opinions on the importance of education. In worship the readers should be located around the room, to give the feeling of movement without actually moving an entire congregation. It is helpful to have the questions for discussion printed in the bulletin; this allows for a smooth transition to discussion time. A large easel with newsprint is needed, to facilitate preparation of the litany.

This service allows for five to seven voices. Including a number of voices in a worship experience gives a feeling of involvement by the congregation and infuses the service with enthusiasm. Since the lines to be read are printed out, a rehearsal is not necessary if readers are thoughtfully chosen.

•

CALL TO WORSHIP

Leader: Look around you friends, look around you:
Who is the person sitting next to you?

Voice 1: The person next to me is the greatest miracle, the greatest mystery I will ever meet — at this moment a live example of the WORD-MADE-FLESH, of God's continuing presence in the world, of God's continuing "coming" into our midst.

Voice 2: The person next to me is an inexhaustible resource of possibilities — and only some of those resources have been tapped.

Voice 3: The person next to me
is a unique universe of experience
is a combination of needs and possibilities,
             dread and desire,
             smiles and frowns,
             laughter and tears,
             fears and hopes,
all struggling to find expression.

Voice 4: The person next to me — is bursting to become something special.
       — to arrive at some destination
       — to have their story known.

Voice 5: The person next to me — has problems and fears
       — wonders "How am I doing?"
       — is often undecided and disorganized, and painfully close to chaos; but is endowed with a great toughness in the face of trouble, able to survive the most unbelievable difficulties.

Leader: But the person next to you can never be fully understood. He or she is more than any description or explanation. For the person next to you is a mystery...as the word made flesh is mystery and dwelt among us. So friends, look around you; for God is here. Let us celebrate!

—Blair Richards and Janice Sigmund,
Come, Let Us Celebrate[1]

HYMN

"Praise Be to God the Almighty," new words by Ruth Duck,
Everflowing Streams

PRAYER OF CONFESSION (unison)

Jesus Christ, we confess to you now
   the wrong things we have done,
   the wrong things we have said,
   the wrong in our hearts.
Please forgive us and help us to live as you want us to. Amen.

— "Prayers to Grow By"[2]

FORGIVENESS AND GOD'S PEACE

Leader: Friends: God knows our needs before we ask. God loves us more than our hearts and minds can imagine. Believe the good news of the Gospel:

People: In Jesus Christ, we are forgiven!

Leader: This is God's house. A place of peace. A place where we befriend one another in the name of Christ.

People: We enter as strangers, we leave as friends.

Leader: Let us greet one another as a sign of God's peace and Christ's friendship. May the peace of Christ be with each of you.

— Rosemary C. Mitchell

WE HEAR THE WORD OF GOD

Job 28:20–28
James 3:13–18

READING: "Finding Wisdom"

Reader 1:   Who is wise and understanding?

Reader 2:   Where does wisdom come from?
How can I find it?

Reader 3:   Wisdom is knowing that you don't know.

Reader 4:   Wisdom comes with age.

Reader 2:   With age? Are you kidding?
Do we know the same people?

Reader 3:   It's the children who are wise,
   all-trusting,
   no inhibitions,
   no prejudices.

Reader 2: But what about being naive and childish?
That's not being wise!

Reader 1: At every age we can learn from experience.
We cannot connect wisdom with age.

Reader 2: Yeah, I know — Ya can't tell 'em a thing —
They have to experience it for themselves.

Reader 1: It's when you begin to listen to that "inner voice"
that is the beginning of wisdom.

Reader 4: Trusting the spirit!

Reader 2: Being open to God!

Reader 3: Understanding paradox!

Reader 1: Living with the tension of the "Already-not-yet!"

Reader 2: It's having more questions than answers!

Reader 3: Wisdom is knowing that all of life teaches us.

Reader 4: Wisdom is realizing that we never stop learning.

—Rosemary C. Mitchell

SHARING THE WORD OF GOD (in pairs)

Answer these questions:

- Who has been your favorite teacher?

- What has been the most difficult thing you have learned in your life?

- How do you describe a wise person?

INTERPRETING THE WORD OF GOD:
"Who Is a Wise Person?"

Worshippers are invited to call out the word they used to describe a wise person. On one sheet of newsprint those words are listed.

The chairperson of Christian Education or the Worship Leader speaks briefly about the demands of the teaching ministry in the life of a congregation and the importance of the gifts of teaching.

DEDICATION OF
CHURCH SCHOOL STAFF

Church School Staff members are invited to come forward at this time.

LITANY OF DEDICATION

The worship leader, using the words on the newsprint, creates a litany with the response: "May God grant you wisdom." At this point the worship leader may speak about the importance of the congregation's support for the teachers and the students throughout the year.

PRAYER OF PARTNERSHIP

Leader: When children live with criticism and impatience they learn that they are not part of Christ's body.

People: May God grant us wisdom.

Leader: When children live with intolerance and are ignored, they wonder why they should be part of Christ's body.

People: May God grant us wisdom.

Leader: When children live with praise and approval they too reflect God's love.

People: May God grant us wisdom.

Leader: When children live with friendliness and understanding they give their energy and enthusiasm.

People: May God grant us wisdom
Amen.

— Dorothy Nolte[3]

HYMN

"Be Thou My Vision," *The Hymnbook*

BLESSING

•

SUGGESTED ALTERNATE HYMNS

"Christ Is Made the Sure Foundation" (TPH, UMH, WB, HB,PH)

"Come, O Thou God of Grace" (WB)

"God Gives His People Strength" (WB)

"God of Grace, God of Glory" (TPH, UMH, WB, HB, PH)

"Holy Spirit, Truth Divine" (TPH, UMH, WB, HB, PH)

"I Sing a Song of the Saints of God" (PH, TPH, UMH)

"Many and Great, O God, Are Thy Things" (TPH, UMH)

"O Splendor of God's Glory Bright" (vs. 1, 2, 3,) (TPH, UMH, WB, HB, PH)

"O God the Creator" (TPH)

"Wellspring of Wisdom" (UMH)

NOTES

1. The Call to Worship is by Blair Richards and Janice Sigmund from *Come, Let Us Celebrate*. © 1976. Hawthorne Press.

2. From *The Lion Book of Children's Prayers*, © 1977 by Lion Publishing Corp. Used by permission. All rights reserved.

3. The Prayer of Partnership is adapted by Dorothy Nolte from "Children Learn What They Live" from *JED SHARE* magazine, © Fall 1979. United Church Press. Used with permission.

23

NEW THINGS
WE NOW DECLARE
(A New Year's Celebration)

INTRODUCTION

Dorothee Sölle, in her book *Beyond Mere Obedience: Reflections on a Christian Ethic for the Future*, describes "phantasie" as an intuitive use of imagination that empowers us to take part in shaping the future.[1] Phantasie, therefore, has to do with *creating* a new and transformed reality — much the same way that an Olympic skier envisions the perfect race in her imagination prior to the event, creating an inner vision of each intricate muscular response. This envisioning effectively prepares the body to *do* the act!

Prediction, on the other hand, has to do with foretelling events based on a *present* reality. Dr. Letty Russell describes this difference in terms of "future shock" and "advent shock." Future shock — profound discontent ("maladjustment") with the present because of a longed-for past — is in direct contrast to "advent shock," which is profound discontent with the present because of a longed-for *future*.[2]

This is a service for the first Sunday of the year. It was originally prepared for "the First Sunday of the Last Decade of the Last Century of the Millennium." It is in that perspective — the vantage point of the broad sweep of time — that we are called to consider our role in helping to bring about "new things."

PREPARATION

Before this service, the leader needs to collect psychics' "new year's predictions," which regularly appear in supermarket tabloids. These should be clipped out or retyped onto 3″ x 5″ cards, enough for every worshipper to be given one upon arrival.

•

RE-MEMBERING GOD'S CALL: Isaiah 42:1

The service begins with participants standing in a circle. Here, each one in turn faces the neighbor to the left, places her hands on the neighbor's shoulders, and announces the words of Isaiah printed below, inserting the name; the corporate response is given after each one is greeted and "blessed" in this way.

> *Each:*   Behold my servant _____, whom I uphold,
>
> *All:*   My chosen, in whom my soul delights...

SONG

Eternal Spirit, We Rely
tune: Truro

> Eternal Spirit, we rely
> On you, to your deeds testify.
> All worlds are yours, all people share
> Creation's pow'r and the choice it bears.
>
> Your love shall guide, your judgments stay,
> Your righteous will direct our way.
> Christ shares our humble, human frame;
> The resurrection we proclaim.
>
> Thus bound in covenant, we search
> For ways to serve you through your church;
> By serving people in their need
> Our lives from self and death are freed.
>
> Your help we seek to face our time,
> Through trial we trust your grace divine.
> Earth's justice, peace, O Church, defend;
> Help shape God's reign which has no end.

—words by Ruth Duck, *Everflowing Streams*[3]

REFLECTION:
Prediction vs. *Phantasie*: Our Prophetic Calling

PREDICTIONS:
...and so we confess...

Each person holding a psychic's "prediction" from a current tabloid is invited to read that prediction. After each reading, all respond together in the manner of a prayer of confession

> We enjoy the status quo. God, forgive us.

HEARING THE WORD

Matthew 3:13–17
Isaiah 42:1–9

RESPONDING TO THE WORD:
"Litany for a New World"

> *All:* Gracious and chastening God,
> we are called to account by the images of your word.
> Something in us groans
> when we realize the tension of our lives,
> between what is and what could be.

> *Right:* You offer us a glimpse of lives set free.
> But we live in a world of bondage,
> where women and men are defined by sinful standards;
> where race, age, and gender
> are weapons used against us,
> rather than gifts.

> *Left:* Giver of life, we see visions and dream dreams —
> but their contrast to the world's reality is stark;
> and so we groan more deeply for a new order.

Silence

> *Leader:* "From the beginning till now the entire creation has
> been groaning in one great act of giving birth; and not
> only creation, but all of us who possess the first-fruits
> of the Spirit, we too groan inwardly as we wait for our
> bodies to be set free." (Rom. 8:22–23)

> *All:* Labor is exhausting.
> How long, O Lord, before we find a resting place?

Silence

> *Leader:* "We were saved by this hope, but in our moments of
> impatience let us remember that hope always means
> waiting for something that we do not yet possess. But
> if we hope for something we cannot see, then we must
> settle down to wait for it in patience." (Rom. 8:24–25)

> *All:* In our birth-pangs we feel anxiety.

> *Right:* At one moment, the Gospel and even our own lives
> seem so long overdue....

> *Left:* But at the next, we fear they may be premature.

All: We confess the frailty of our hope,
the hesitance of our purpose.
Strong and merciful God,
startle us awake to the certainty of our calling.

Silence

Leader: "The Spirit of God not only maintains this hope within
us, but helps us in our present limitations. We do not
know how to pray worthily as children of God, but the
Spirit within us is actually praying for us in those ag-
onizing longings which never find words...." (Rom.
8:26–27)

All: Remind us that we do not groan in isolation —
but together, and with your whole creation.
When we would shirk from pain, recall us.
When we grow weak, renew us with your spirit.

Our own spirits are birthing, Lord.
In silence now we offer you
what already lies hidden within us,
conceived and nurtured by your love....

Silence

Leader: Creator, Redeemer, Sustainer,
through the groanings of this task
we know you are with us.

Right: With the pain we sense a great surge of power.

Left: In the shedding of lifeblood, we are strengthened.

All: According to your promise
we watch and work for new heavens and a new earth,
in which labor will be over
and all things born into freedom.

Alleluia! So let it be!

— Gail A. Ricciuti

PHANTASIE:
...by which we proclaim...

Here participants are invited to express a prophetic phantasie *that envisions
a transformation in the world. After each is spoken, one voice leads and all
respond with this affirmation:*

One: "Behold, the former things have come to pass,

All: And new things we now declare."

SONG

"O For a World," *The Presbyterian Hymnal*

SHARING THE FEAST...

Words of Invitation: Sisters and brothers, we come to this table with advent shock, profoundly uncomfortable with the present because of a longed-for future promised by God. It is in these common things, this bread and this cup, that we behold a world transformed, a new and holy reality dawning in our lives. Let us gather around the table for that feast!

Prayers

Here bidding prayers may be used, inviting the gathered community to pray either silently or aloud for common concerns.

Words of Institution

Sharing the Bread and the Cup

PRAYER OF THANKSGIVING

For all things bright and beautiful,
For all things dark and mysterious and lovely,
For all things green and growing and strong,
For all things weak and struggling to push life up through rocky earth,
For all human faces, hearts, minds, and hands which surround us,
And for all nonhuman minds and hearts, paws and claws, fins and
    wings,
For this Life and the life of this world,
For all that you have laid before us, O God,
We lay our thankful hearts before you. In Christ's name,
    Amen.

—Gail A. Ricciuti

SONG

"Spirit"; words by Ruth Duck in *Everflowing Streams*

BENEDICTION

SUGGESTED ALTERNATE HYMNS

"Hymn of Promise" (UMH)

"Live into Hope" (TPH)

"Shall We Gather at the River" (UMH)

NOTES

1. Dorothee Sölle, in her book *Beyond Mere Obedience: Reflections on a Christian Ethic for the Future* (Minneapolis: Augsburg, 1970), p. 10.

2. See Letty Russell, *The Future of Partnership* (Philadelphia: Westminster Press, 1979), pp. 101–3.

3. Adapted words for "Eternal Spirit, We Rely," used by permission as published in *Everflowing Streams* by Ruth Duck, 1980, United Church Press, 1974 and 1981, New York.

PART III

A Retreat for Women

24

POWER, LOVE,
AND A SOUND MIND

(based on 2 Timothy 1:5–7)

INTRODUCTION

Fearfulness is a significant spiritual and social issue for women in our culture. Crime statistics teach us that we dare never take it for granted that we are altogether safe on the street. From childhood, our mothers taught us certain rules for survival because we were female, and those recorded themselves like a mantra in the depths of our consciousness: Do not walk alone at night...hang on to your purse...be courteous but *don't* speak to strangers...lower your eyes when approaching strange men, but always be alert....The contradictions inherent in these cautions often created a tightrope of dissonance in us.

We also learned timidity because of our gender: Better to downplay your intelligence...ladies never make the first move...don't speak up for yourself and risk giving offense...it is up to us to keep the peace...anger is dangerous. The rules we internalize with the air we breathe serve to cripple our spirits, hobbling us as if we walked on tiny, bound feet. Recent research by Dr. Carol Gilligan is yielding unexpected data concerning the psychological development of young girls that underscores the detrimental effect of timidity in women's lives: Girls up to approximately eleven years of age experience a healthy integration of integrity and intimacy, asserting themselves freely and expressing feelings openly without fear of conflict. In adolescence, however, girls begin to lose confidence in their own voices and feelings, to fear that their opinions will anger others, and to silence themselves in favor of "acting nice." The challenge for women, Gilligan theorizes, is not (as formerly thought) to *reach* a developmental stage of strength and autonomy, but to reclaim something we have lost.[1] We need to recover our identity as authorities on our own experience.

175

Theologically and spiritually, the message of the Gospel is that the "spirit of fear" or "spirit of timidity" is not God's intention for whole human beings; rather, the divine gifts *already* in our grasp are "power, love, and a sound mind [self-control]." With that in mind, we set out on this retreat to "re-empower" each other to let go of fear and reclaim our strength!

PREPARATION

Supplies and resources needed:

- Five sets of index cards with ten cards in a set (each set a different color)
- Marking pens and writing pens
- Large candle in a holder (a Paschal candle is recommended; but a fireplace or campfire can be used)
- Galvanized garbage can or burning barrel
- Rope (at least thirty feet)
- Clothesline and clothespins
- Paper plates, construction paper, markers, masking tape, and other supplies for mask making
- Scissors
- Cassette tape player
- Bibles
- Decks of "Great Women" biographical cards,[2] with ten women represented per deck, enough decks so that each participant can be matched with one "Great Woman." There are three different decks, which may all be used in this retreat: "Founders and Firsts," "Fore-mothers," and "Poets and Writers." For each woman pictured, there are additional cards in the deck giving significant facts about her life and achievement, and quoting her words. In preparation for the retreat, each deck must be divided into individual envelopes, each of which will contain the cards for a single character.

Note regarding retreat schedule: This retreat is designed to run from Friday evening to Saturday afternoon. Mealtimes, coffee breaks, or "breathers" between sections have not been suggested in the retreat plan, so that groups can determine their own appropriate pace. One possibility is to begin the program at 7 or 7:30 in the evening, with late snacks served at the end of Part III; begin the Saturday segments with a light continental breakfast, and then break after

Part V for a late-morning brunch. Patterned this way, the retreat ends by mid-afternoon. With a more leisurely pace, the retreat can be adapted to an entire weekend, beginning Friday evening and ending by Sunday noon, with recreational or other activities added to the experience.

•

FRIDAY EVENING
Part I (one hour)

WELCOME AND INTRODUCTION
TO RETREAT SCHEDULE AND FACILITIES

COMMUNITY BUILDING

1. Participants, in circles of ten, introduce themselves and answer the question "What were you doing between 1 and 3 o'clock this afternoon?"

2. Use the game "Knots" as a way of getting "unknotted" from the week:

Knots

This game is drawn from *The New Games Book*,[3] where a complete description may be found. It is an intriguing exercise in which every group "wins." Groups of nine to twelve players are ideal. To form the knot, players stand in a circle, shoulder-to-shoulder, placing their hands in the center. Each person is instructed to grab two other hands; but no one should hold both hands with the same person, or with a person immediately on either side of her. When the knot is formed, the group's task is to untangle themselves without breaking their grip. Players must often step over and under others' arms (pivoting handholds helps to avoid dislocated joints!). Amazingly, when the knot is finally unraveled the group will find itself, without fail, either in one large circle or, occasionally, in two interlocking ones. The cheer that goes up at the end of the task is always spontaneous!

3. Have groups "debrief" the game for a few minutes. Ask them to compare this experience with the experience of their own life's work. What did they learn about others in the group in the process?

Part II *(one hour)*
FACING OUR FEARS

Have the participants form groups of no more than seven. Ask one person in each group to serve as facilitator. This person is given a list of questions for group discussion.

1. Each person chooses a colored index card from a basket and is asked to list on the card ten things she fears most.

2. Cards are collected.

3. Leader shuffles cards into a basket.

4. Cards are redistributed, one to each person.

5. The women are asked to form five groups according to color of the cards.

6. In these groupings, each woman reads aloud the fears listed on the card in her hand.

7. Group discussion (allow 20–30 minutes):

   • What similarities do you recognize in the lists?

   • How do these fears relate to being a woman?

   • Which fears are most limiting to women's power?

Part III *(30–45 minutes)*
THE MASK OF FEAR

Each woman is given supplies to make a "fear" mask, and asked to create a representation (with eye-holes) of her "fearful face."

After masks are made, invite the group to form one large circle, each participant holding her mask in front of her face so that she can peer through the eye-holes to look at others' masks.

Ask the group to ponder, in silence, what patterns and/or similarities they notice among the masks.

One voice then reads the following poem:

I

I go among trees and sit still.
All my stirring becomes quiet
around me like circles on water.
My tasks lie in their places
where I left them, asleep like cattle.

Then what is afraid of me comes
and lives a while in my sight.
What it fears in me leaves me,
and the fear of me leaves it.
It sings, and I hear its song.

Then what I am afraid of comes.
I live for a while in its sight.
What I fear in it leaves it,
and the fear of it leaves me.
It sings, and I hear its song.

After days of labor,
mute in my consternations,
I hear my song at last,
and I sing it. As we sing
the day turns, the trees move.

— Wendell Berry, *Sabbaths*[4]

There follows a ritual of embracing and blessing one another and putting our fears to rest, in which participants hang their masks on a line(s) hung across one end of the meeting space.

SATURDAY MORNING
Part IV (one hour)
TRANSFORMING FEARS INTO POWER

INTRODUCTORY REFLECTIONS

Scripture: 2 Timothy 1:5–7

Here the leader may also want to reflect on the relationship of fear to power in her own experience as a way of introducing the morning's program.

Reading

And Miriam rose before sunrise, while Moses and Aaron and all the sons of men were yet asleep. In the faint moonlight she could see the shapes of other women moving quietly to kindle cookfires and she was filled with a strange, unutterable sadness. And on the wind a voice came to her, soothing and gentle and calling her name.

"Miriam. Miriam."

"Mother? Mother Goddess, is it you?"

"It is I, my child."

And lo, it was as though a loving hand touched Miriam's cheek, and Miriam, the prophetess, began to weep.

"How did you find me here, in this barren desert, this wasted place, where women and children die and all are hungry?"

"I always know where you are, my daughter, and I love you." Miriam smiled and dried her eyes on the sleeve of her robe.

"Is there something you would require of me, my Mother?"

"Yes, my child. I see Moses writing half truths on clay tablets and I wonder, where are the writings of my daughter Miriam?"

"Oh, Mother, I have no time for writing on clay tablets. That is for Moses to do. He wanders in the wilderness for days at a time. He has no one he serves, no goats and sheep to tend, no sick infants to care for, no cloth to weave nor repair, no dying to comfort, no babes to bring into the world . . . "

"I know, my daughter, and yet, if only Moses leaves a record, who will know of your struggle, your duties, your strength, how you made freedom possible?"

"Moses will write of it."

"Will he? I know what Moses writes of you my child. Shall I tell you?"

"Yes, my Mother, for he knows that I and all the women have kept us from starvation, lo, these forty years. We have made habitable those places where no creature can live, and we have survived."

"Hear, my child, the words of Moses: 'And Miriam, the prophetess, the sister of Aaron, took a timbrel in her hand and all the women went out after her with timbrels and danced.' " Miriam was silent for a long time.

"That is all he says of me?"

"Yes, my child."

"After I saved him from being slain by Pharaoh, after this perilous journey, after I lifted the hearts of the weary so that they could continue with hope when strength was gone. After all these things . . . "

"Yes child, after all these things. And I say unto you, who will speak for the women? How will your daughters know of your suffering and your strength it they have only Moses' words? When will you speak for yourself and your sisters?" The dawn was breaking now and Miriam arose.

"When I have time, my Mother, I will write our women's story upon the clay tablets. It is time for me to go now, to prepare the breakfast and to fold the tents . . . but as soon as I have time . . . as soon as I have time. . . . "

— Sharon Hatton, A Scriptural Invention

Prayer

> Inhabit our hearts,
> God of history,
> as You once inhabited
> human flesh.
> Be here among us
> with all of Your wisdom,
> all of Your power,
> all of Your mercy,
> all of Your love,
> that we might learn
> to be like God
> from our God who came
> to be like us.
> Holy are You.
> Holy are we
> who are one with You forever.
> Amen.

— Miriam Therese Winter,
WomanPrayer, WomanSong[5]

WHAT IS YOUR GIFT?:
Power, Love, or a Sound Mind?

Group conversation on the meaning of power.

1. Have women reflect momentarily on which gift they feel is theirs.

2. Take a poll: how many feel they have which gift? A common experience is that very few in groups composed of women claim power as a gift they recognize in themselves. If this proves true in your group, the observation should be noted at this time.

3. Why do so few claim power as a gift? Ask for responses from the group as a whole.

4. A brief presentation by one of the leaders about power: women's power, personal power, professional power.

Background

In our time the psychologist Rollo May has identified five kinds of power. Each of them is an exercise for contemplation and ... a challenge to Christianity itself.

May tells us that every act of power is either exploitative, competitive, manipulative, integrative or nurturing. Exploitation, competition, and manipulation, May teaches us, are powers used to destroy. Exploitative power is "power over" another. Competitive power is power used "against another." Manipulative power is power used to "control another" secretly, legally, dishonestly. We use power to defeat and control people, until finally, by destroying them, we destroy ourselves, our world, our institutions, our very souls.

Power used to target the globe for extinction is certainly destructive, exploitative power. Power used to rape the environment — to poison the water and pollute the environment of this globe — is power run amok! Power amassed to protect the Church from eleven-year-old altar girls, and the erotic feet of women, and the use of feminine pronouns in the midst of a poor world is power gone inane. Power used to suppress thinkers in a culture and an era that is more dominated by questions than by answers is a worthless use of power that will do more, in the end, to harm us than the questions ever could.

These kinds of power are crying for a spirituality that empowers; for a power that pleads and a power that frees. For a power that's gentle, and a power that cares for the people; for power that empowers others.

Nurturing power and integrative power, May insists, are the only hope for our times. We need a government, we need a people, we need a Church, with a massive, overwhelming reservoir of power to bring people to life and the world together.

— Joan Chittister, from
"Empowerment and Spirituality"[6]

5. Small group discussion. Again invite one person to serve as facilitator in each group.
   Questions for discussion:

   - What images come to mind when you think of power?
   - Are they positive or negative images for you?
   - All of us *do have* power. Where is the power in you? Name *your* power.
   - Which fears stop or limit your power?
   - When and where do you give away your power?
   - What is the source of your power?

Part V (one hour)
DESTROYING OUR FEARS

We have discovered that when a woman grasps the power that is within her, her fears turn to ashes; and when her fears become ashes, that is further empowering!

Invite each participant to claim her fear mask from the line where it has hung since the night before. Move outdoors for a ritual of "burning our fears" to symbolize the end of their power as they turn to ashes. (It is most effective to gather around a lighted Paschal candle on a stand, symbolizing the powerful light of the risen Christ; but a bonfire may be used for the ritual, or an indoor fireplace in inclement weather. Outdoors, a large galvanized garbage can or burning barrel should be placed in proximity to the candle; indoors, it would be wise to have a bucket of water nearby for fire safety.)

When the group has formed a circle around the Christ fire, the following reading may be presented, with different voices alternating portions of the poem:

For Strong Women [7]

A strong woman is a woman who is straining.
A strong woman is a woman standing
on tiptoe and lifting a barbell
while trying to sing Boris Godunov.
A strong woman is a woman at work
cleaning out the cesspool of the ages,
and while she shovels, she talks about
how she doesn't mind crying, it opens
the ducts of the eyes, and throwing up
develops the stomach muscles, and
she goes on shoveling with tears
   in her nose.

A strong woman is a woman in whose head
a voice is repeating, I told you so,
ugly, bad girl, bitch, nag, shrill, witch,
ballbuster, nobody will ever love you back,
why aren't you feminine, why aren't
you soft, why aren't you quiet, why
aren't you dead?

A strong woman is a woman determined
to do something others are determined
not be done. She is pushing up on the bottom
of a lead coffin lid. She is trying to raise
a manhole cover with her head, she is trying
to butt her way through a steel wall.
Her head hurts. People waiting for the hole
to be made say, hurry, you're so strong.

A strong woman is a woman bleeding
inside. A strong woman is a woman making
herself strong every morning while her teeth
loosen and her back throbs. Every baby,

a tooth, midwives used to say, and now
every battle a scar. A strong woman
is a mass of scar tissue that aches
when it rains and wounds that bleed
when you bump them and memories that get up
in the night and pace in boots to and fro.

A strong woman is a woman who craves love
like oxygen or she turns blue choking.
A strong woman is a woman who loves
strongly and weeps strongly and is strongly
terrified and has strong needs. A strong woman is strong
in words, in action, in connection, in feeling;
she is not strong as a stone but as a wolf
suckling her young. Strength is not in her, but she
enacts it as the wind fills a sail.

What comforts her is others loving
her equally for the strength and for the weakness
from which it issues, lightning from a cloud.
Lightning stuns. In rain, the clouds disperse.
Only water of connection remains,
flowing through us. Strong is what we make
each other. Until we are all strong together,
a strong woman is a woman strongly afraid.

— Marge Piercy, *The Moon Is Always Female*

Here a leader invites participants to step forward when they are ready to let go of their fears into the light of Christ; to light the edge of their "fear mask" in the flame of the Paschal candle; and, as the flame spreads across the mask, to drop it into the burning barrel placed nearby (or, if a fireplace is used, to place the mask in the flames). Reminding them of the words of 2 Timothy 1:7 (RSV: "for God did not give us a spirit of timidity but a spirit of power and love and self-control"; KJV: "For God hath not given us the spirit of fear, but of power, and of love, and of a sound mind"), the leader invites each to choose *one* of the following affirmations and to proclaim it aloud as she sets her fears afire:

"My power overcomes fear."
"My love overcomes fear."
"My sound mind [self-control] overcomes fear."

Part VI (90 minutes)

In his second letter to Timothy, Paul writes "I am reminded of your sincere faith, a faith that dwelt first in your grandmother Lois and your mother Eunice and now, I am sure, dwells in you" (2 Tim. 1:5). In times of our early faith development, or at junctures of crisis or timidity in life, we sometimes "come through" simply by having faith in someone *else's* faith until we are strong enough to stand on a faith of our own. (As some have said, faith is more often *caught* than *taught*!) Fear itself is sometimes overcome by recalling the power and fearlessness of our "grandmothers in faith" and our "mothers in faith." In this retreat, time is therefore set aside to recall and celebrate this sacred, empowering memory of our "grandmothers" (defined for this purpose as women who went before us, whom we never *personally* knew) and our "mothers" (women who may be related to us or not, now living *or* deceased, but who have passed through and blessed our own lives).

"LOIS": The Power of Our Grandmothers

A large basket is passed around the group, full of the envelopes containing the Great Women cards. Each participant draws one envelope. In small groups again, the following process is suggested:

1. In silence, each person contemplates the information and personality on her cards — not only reading the words, but studying the face and quietly seeking to "get a feel" for who this woman was.

2. One by one, each "introduces" her character to the rest of the group, summarizing her life and accomplishment. (This process in itself has proven a fascinating one for groups of women who find themselves learning women's history and contributions to society previously unknown to them.)

3. Each participant then is asked to reflect aloud, briefly, on these questions:

- What kinship do I feel with this woman? What is it that we have in common, she and I?

- What new strength or power do I learn from her, or in what existing strength do I feel affirmed by her?

The "matching" of group participants with historical grandmothers in this way may appear arbitrary at first; but it has been our experience that the Spirit works in mysterious ways, even in such an exercise, and that without fail, profound connections are discovered when the envelopes are opened. For some women, this has been the most significant (even life-changing) part of the retreat.

"EUNICE": The Influence of Our Mothers in Faith

At this point, small groups are gathered back into one large circle, around a worship center that has already been prepared (see instructions below). This final portion of Part VI is most effectively done as a bridge leading directly into the Closing Worship.

A length of pliable (1/4 to 1/2 inch) rope is passed from person to person [thirty feet is a minimum length for a group of fifty to sixty women]. Each, in turn, ties a knot in the rope as she names a living "mother" of hers in the faith, identifying in a sentence or two why that woman has been influential in her life. When all have knotted the rope, it is spread out on the floor to encircle the worship center or table.

CLOSING WORSHIP
(30 minutes)

PREPARATION

A low table draped with a white cloth is set up as a worship center in the middle of the room. On the table are placed common objects such as a box of tissue, coffee mug, newspaper, Bible, stapler, candle, yellow legal pad, pop can, cooking pot, basket, teddy bear, baby bonnet, clay pot, sea shells, bread on a plate, flowers, an embroidered handkerchief.

GATHERING WORDS

Voice 1:   We told our stories —
That's All.

Voice 2:   We sat and listened to
Each other

Voice 3:   And heard the journeys
Of Each soul.

Voice 4:   We sat in silence
Entering each one's pain and
Sharing each one's joy.

Voice 5:   We heard love's longing
And the lonely reachings-out
For love and affirmation.

Voice 6:   We heard of dreams
Shattered.
And visions fled.
Of hopes and laughter
Turned stale and dark.

Voice 7: We felt the pain of
Isolation and
The bitterness
Of death.

All: But in each brave and
Lonely story
God's gentle life
Broke through
And we heard music in
The darkness
And smelt flowers in
The void.

Voice 1: We felt the budding
Of creation
In the searchings of
Each soul
And discerned the beauty
Of God's hand in
Each muddy, twisted path.

Voice 2: And God's voice sang
In each story
Christ's life sprang from
Each death.

Voice 3: Our sharing became
One story
Of a simple lonely search
For life and hope and
Oneness
In a world which sobs
For love.

All: And we knew that in
Our sharing God's voice with
Mighty breath
Was saying
Love each other and
Take each other's hand

Voice 4: For you are one
Though many
And in each of you
I live.
So listen to my story

And share my pain
And death.
Oh, listen to my story
And rise and live
With me.

— Edwina Gately, "The Sharing,"
Psalms of a Laywoman[8]

SONG

"Great Creator God, You Call Us," by Jane Parker Huber,
in *A Singing Faith*

REFLECTION AND DISCUSSION

Participants are asked to focus on the familiar objects displayed in the
worship center, choose one object, and to think about how that object
is a symbol of her life experience. After a time of silence each is invited
to share her thoughts with a woman sitting next to her.

A LITANY OF POWER, LOVE, AND STRONG MINDS

Leader: God of our years, our lives are in your hands. We remember today our foremothers, who throughout time
have used their gifts of power, love, and the strong
minds you gave them to change the world. We call
upon these foremothers to help us discover within
ourselves our gifts.

All: We remember SARAH, a strong woman of faith who
answered God's call to forsake her homeland and to
put her faith in the promises and covenant of God.

Leader: We pray for her power of faith.

All: We remember ESTHER, DEBORAH, and RAHAB, who
by acts of individual courage saved their people.

Leader: We pray for their sound minds and courage acting for
the greater good.

All: We remember MARY MAGDALENE, JOHANNA, MARY,
and the other women who followed Jesus and who
were not believed when they announced the resurrection.

Leader: We pray for their love and faith in the face of skepti-
cism.

All: We remember PHOEBE, PRISCILLA, and all the women leaders of the early church.

Leader: We pray for their power and sound minds that spread the Gospel and inspired congregations.

All: We pray for the love and sound minds of women who are first in their field.

Leader: We pray for their power of leadership and their sound minds.

All: May they be granted the power and sound minds as they open up new possibilities for all women.

Leader: We pray for our daughters and granddaughters.

All: May they be granted the power, love, and strong minds to seek that life which is uniquely theirs.
We have celebrated our power.
We have celebrated our love.
We have celebrated our strong minds.
We have been given these gifts from God.
Our bodies touch in love,
Our mouths speak words of power,
Our search for truth and justice
reflect our strong minds.
Spirit of God be with us in our touching,
our speaking, our searching.
Amen.

—Ann Heidkamp,
from *No Longer Strangers*[9]

•

NOTES

1. Carol Gilligan, Nona P. Lyons, Trudy J. Hamner, eds., *Making Connections: The Relational Worlds of Adolescent Girls at Emma Willard School* (Cambridge, Mass.: Harvard University Press, 1990).

2. "Great Women," a biographical card game by Aristoplay, Ltd., P.O. Box 7028, Ann Arbor, MI 48107. © 1979.

3. "Knots," from *The New Games Book*, edited by Andrew Fluegelman. © 1976 by The Headlands Press, Inc.

4. "I," by Wendell Berry, from *Sabbaths*, published by North Point Press. Reprinted with permission.

5. "Inhabit Our Hearts..." is by Miriam Therese Winter and is from *WomanPrayer, WomanSong*.

6. Excerpt from "Empowerment and Spirituality," by Joan Chittister, as printed in *Creation* 6, no. 2, 1990. Reprinted by permission of author.

7. "For Strong Women," from *The Moon Is Always Female*, by Marge Piercy. © 1980 by Marge Piercy. Reprinted by permission of Alfred A. Knopf, Inc.

8. "The Sharing," by Edwina Gately from *Psalms of a Laywoman*, published by Source Books. Used with permission of author.

9. Closing litany by Ann Heidkamp, from *No Longer Strangers: A Resource for Women and Worship*, by Iben Gjerding and Katherine Kinnamon. © 1983, World Council of Churches Publication, P.O. Box 2100, 1211 Geneva 2, Switzerland. Used by permission.

AFTERWORD

"I took the road less traveled by, and that made all the difference" mused the American poet laureate Robert Frost. Our "Women, Word, and Song" community indeed walks a less-traveled road. It is an expression of the longing of a great many women for a way to understand and worship God that can integrate a deep spirituality with a commitment to inclusiveness in the church and justice in the world. We hunger for worship to be a transforming experience adequate to sustain us in the life of faith.

We know the journey is just beginning. As we discover and create new ways of naming God, women who share in such empowerment have, both figuratively and literally, changed their names. Others who were formerly convinced that the Christian church was a dead institution for *their* lives have with joyous disbelief found themselves "welcomed home."

Finally, the two of us who have co-authored this book rejoice as well — not only in the great Good News that is finding voice in women's faith community, but in the rare blessing of working side by side as colleagues and trusted friends. May this Liberation Road carry us all to a horizon beyond our farthest vision!